D1600710

Mirages on the Sea of Time

MIRAGES ON
The Taoist

EDWARD H. SCHAFER

THE SEA OF TIME
Poetry of Ts'ao T'ang

UNIVERSITY OF CALIFORNIA PRESS

BERKELEY • LOS ANGELES • LONDON

University of California Press
Berkeley and Los Angeles, California

University of California Press, Ltd.
London, England

© 1985 by
The Regents of the University of California

Printed in the United States of America

1 2 3 4 5 6 7 8 9

Library of Congress Cataloging in Publication Data

Schafer, Edward H.
  Mirages on the sea of time.

  Bibliography: p.
  Includes index.
  1. Ts'ao, T'ang, fl. 847-873—Criticism and
interpretation.   I. Title.
  PL2677.T65Z88   1985   895.1′13   84-24132
  ISBN 0-520-05429-6

TO PHYLLIS BROOKS

Contents

INTRODUCTION   1
Mao Shan   2
Taoist Poets of T'ang   7
Poetic Forms with Taoist Content   11
Terminology   16
Translations   26

PART I: TS'AO T'ANG AND HIS ELYSIAN   31
           ENCOUNTERS

PART II: PRINCIPALITIES OF THE SEA   49
           P'eng-lai   51
           The Hollow Worlds   61
           Jade Consorts and Pelagic Costumes 66
           Clam Castles and the Fata Morgana   80
           Miss Hemp   90
           Fu-sang   103
           Blue Lad and the Fang-chu Palace   108

           Notes   123
           Bibliographies   137
           Glossaries   143
           Index   147

INTRODUCTION

THIS IS A BOOK about a ninth-century Chinese poet, Ts'ao T'ang, and his particular visions of Taoist realms on earth and in the sky. The vanished world in which he lived and the ways of thought that inspired him are little known today, even in China. But with some knowledge and effort of the imagination, we can enter his world. This introduction provides, in capsule form, a quick overview of the medieval Taoist religion, and some of the poets and poetic forms most influenced by it. Since some of the words used in the book are necessarily rare, or are used in unfamiliar contexts, the last part of the introduction is a guide to their meaning, often not easily reduced to one or two English words. With this background, the reader will be ready to meet the elegant and mystifying Ts'ao T'ang.

He has redeemed
The body's dignity
In its own name:
Its rubied arteries,
Its orient mines
Of breath and eyes,
Its nerves like chains
Of lapis lazuli.

KENNETH SCHOLES,
"Recovery"

Mao Shan

UNTIL QUITE RECENTLY most westerners accepted a conventional and quite artificial notion of Taoism, largely based on the revulsion of the Manchus, rulers of China from the seventeenth to the twentieth century, against what they regarded as the dangerous superstitions of the people they had conquered. They denigrated this native Chinese religion, with its complex pantheon, its consecrated priesthood, its rituals and disciplines, and the rich literature it had generated. In time they were successful in persuading the Chinese literate classes that true adherence to the Tao was not religious at all, but consisted in quietistic attitudes and activities, the harmless admiration of nature, and reverence for a few very ancient books, notably the *Lao tzu*, with its ambiguous gnosis and elastic paradoxes, and the *Chuang tzu*, full of fables, fantasies, and cosmic parables. These texts belong to the age of nascent Taoism. Later they provided a substantial body of imagery to the enrichment of the sacred scriptures of the established Taoist faith, which began its long career around the beginning of our era. Fertilized by the old immortality cult, it welcomed the official deification of Lao Tzu as creator, teacher, and savior, and achieved a structure and social role as a salvationist church, dominated by the Heavenly Masters of the Chang family.

In the course of time, an immense corpus of canonical literature was accumulated. We know it as the *Tao tsang*, "The Hoard of the Tao." It contains scriptures, revelations, ritual texts, hagiographies, alchemical procedures, physiological disciplines, magical spells, theology, cosmology, metaphysics, ethics, and poetry as they were realized in the books of the several schools, traditions, and sects of all periods of Chinese history, then modified, harmonized, edited, decorated, and published as a large and diversified whole. Until very recently hardly any western scholar, or eastern for that matter, had been willing to exhaust his time and energy in the study of this great compilation, accepting cheerfully (and thankfully) the assurance of the complacent Mandarins that it was all nonsense anyhow. It was as if the Bible had been rejected as ignoble in Christian lands, the Qur'an throughout Islam, or the whole body of Indian religious literature, including the Buddhist scriptures, elsewhere in Asia, Fortunately this stultifying tradition is now withering, and each year first-rate scholars are giving more of their attention to the study of Taoism as it really was in the lives, thoughts, and writings of the Chinese at different stages of their cultural development. Learned journals now publish pioneering articles on such subjects as ancient techniques for absorbing astral energies, the Taoist theocracies of Northern Wei (fifth century) and of Sung (twelfth century), the ecstatic poetry of Taoist priests, the meaning and purpose of the great rituals, and so on. Soon, it appears, the writing of uninformed paraphrases and private interpretations of the ambiguous text of *Lao tzu*—long a popular pastime regarded as "Taoist studies"—will be entirely the concern of dabblers, while the exciting work of mining the neglected riches of Taoist history and thought will occupy the forefront of Chinese studies for generations to come.

During T'ang times, the age of the poet Ts'ao T'ang, the Taoist religion was a spiritual force of enormous cultural significance, and the dynasty promoted it as an indispensible mainstay. Two bodies of Taoist belief and practice, hardly antagonistic enough to be considered denominational rivals and in many ways complementary, had come to prevail, although other Taoist traditions had their own followers, texts, and peculiar disciplines. The more public of the two is known as Ling Pao and the more private as Mao Shan. The latter persuasion is named for a mountain near Nanking where its basic scriptures were revealed in the 4th century and its tenets codified in the 5th. It is also known as the Taoism of Highest Clarity (*Shang Ch'ing*). The poetry of Ts'ao T'ang must be understood largely within the context of the Mao Shan system.

Early in the fourth century, when invading nomads drove the ruling classes from their northern homeland, the ancient "Middle Kingdom," the refugees were forced to adapt themselves to the provincial manners but pleasant surroundings of the lower Yangtze Valley. The religious traditions they brought with them were gradually integrated with some features of indigenous southern cults—particularly those which emphasized physiological and mental disciplines and engaged in refined alchemical practices.

In the T'ang era, the Taoism of the Highest Clarity school, which had emerged triumphant from this amalgam, claimed as its Mecca, Jerusalem, and Rome the triple peaks of Mount Mao, not far from Nanking and named for Lord Mao Ying, the eponymous founder of the religion. Believers in its tenets visited the place whenever possible and often established private residences on its slopes, adjacent to its holy relics and busy shrines.

Salvation and apotheosis depended on the assiduous practice of carefully defined disciplines and austerities, leading to private visions of deities—usually of the opposite sex—who, in the form of divine lovers, transmitted holy books revealing the road to eternal life among the stars. These written arcana were regarded as imperfect copies of ineffable originals in the celestial archives, which the lucky adept might hope to see, pure and uncorrupted, after his elevation. Since the attainment of these goals required long application, longevity was a pre-condition of success. Accordingly there was much emphasis on diet, hygiene, knowledge of demonifuges, the compounding of mineral elixirs, and physiological techniques, all aimed at postponing death so that release from the corruptible body could precede its actual dissolution. All of these beliefs and practices were modeled into an organic whole, whose heart was the doctrine of "correspondences," that is, the confidence that each vital organ, itself a photophore, was in a state of sympathetic vibration with a shining deity or an asterism. This belief extended to sets of equivalents in nature, music, alchemy, and so on. The great scripture, central to all Highest Clarity activities, was the ancient "Scripture of the Yellow Court" (*Huang t'ing ching*) in which the identity of the spirits inhabiting the human body with great astral divinities is elucidated. These deities could be actualized—made palpable and visible to the accomplished adept—in such internal chambers as the Hall of Light (*Ming T'ang*) in the cranium, or in the scarlet cavities of the heart. With this point-for-point harmony between the microcosm and the macrocosm achieved, the aspirant for eternity was prepared to absorb vital energies radiated by the stars and planets, sometimes transmitted to him directly, if he was a man, from the ardent mouth of a jade maiden, his divine preceptress and spouse; comparable techniques were available to female adepts. This astral emphasis was reflected in a complex stellar pantheon, and expressed outwardly by rites addressed to the stellar powers, who were, in fact, celestial magicians who held the secrets of eternal life. These ceremonies normally began at midnight on remote alpine stages, preferably near caverns leading to subterranean spirit-worlds, and concluded with the dawn, when the rosy fingers of the life-giving sun pierced the eastern sky. These and other techniques of devotion and self-discipline could ultimately lead to the formation of an immortal child—the reduced, purified, and immortalized ego of the aspirant—destined to escape forever from its corruptible husk and rise to partake of the indescribable delights of life in the blue and gold fields of the sky.

Usque adeo caeli respondet pagina nostrae,
  Astrorum et nexus syllaba scripta refert.

ANDREW MARVELL,
  "*Illustrissimo viro Domino Lanceloto Josepho de Maniban Grammatomanti.*"

So much does the page of the heavens
  correspond to ours,
And the written syllable refer to the patterns of
  the stars.

Taoist Poets of T'ang

SUCH WAS THE RELIGIOUS TRADITION familiar to educated men of the T'ang period, and the background against which much T'ang poetry becomes intelligible.

The writers of Taoist literature are not very well known now, except for a few in whose works Taoist themes appear only sporadically: Li Po is a case in point. The rejection by the doyens of Chinese literary history of writing inspired by "superstitious Taoism" has for a long time been complete. But now it appears that the resultant gap in our understanding of medieval literature will quickly be

7

repaired. Long-standing anti-Taoist prejudices are eroding rapidly, even though most of the work of restoration remains to be done. Here I will draw attention to the names of only some of these neglected writers, other than Ts'ao T'ang, the subject of this study, and briefly adumbrate some part of their contribution. Many others who wrote of the roads to the stars remain to be studied and appreciated.

Szu-ma Ch'eng-chen (647–735), the "Twelfth Mao Shan Patriarch," had his retreat on Mount Wang Wu but also maintained close ties with Mount T'ien T'ai. He was also a teacher of kings. His studies of magic swords and mirrors survive in the canon.[1]

Li Po (701–762) was the famous "Grand White" who merged his identity both with the planet Venus and with the Wine Star (in our Leo). He had visions of meeting snow-white jade maidens in remote mountain forests. Indeed, he was formally initiated into some celestial secrets.[2]

Wu Yün (?–778), the acknowledged peer of his close friend Li Po, wrote glittering verses—"subtle" and "miraculous"—expressing the essence of Highest Clarity, and traced the highroads through the stars to the heart of the cosmos.[3]

Yen Chen-ch'ing (709–784), a learned courtier under several monarchs, was noted as a calligrapher in the cursive "grass" style. Few of his poems survive, but a considerable body of elegant prose is extant, notably memorial inscriptions, some of which are contributions to Taoist hagiography.[4]

Ku K'uang (ca. 725–ca. 814), a gentleman-hermit of Mao Shan, was a lover of nature, an initiate into Taoist mysteries, and a true craftsman of celestial language.[5]

Wei Ch'ü-mou (749–801), first a Taoist priest, became a

Buddhist monk, then a collator in the royal library. Eventually, because of his learning and eloquence, he attained high rank at court. Only a few of his poems survive, among them nineteen "Cantos on Pacing the Void." These are richly figured pictures of the difficulties of the search for eternal life, but do not aim at the high ecstatic level which Wu Yün developed under the same rubric.[6]

Hsüeh T'ao (768–831), was a professional entertainer and companion of celebrated writers and statesmen, Yüan Chen above all, but also Po Chü-i, P'ei Tu, Tu Mu, and Liu Yü-hsi. She was a native of Ch'ang-an, then a resident of Ch'eng-tu. Late in life she retired as a Taoist priestess. She achieved some fame as a designer and maker of writing papers.[7]

Hsü Hun (fl. 844), a writer on both Buddhist and Taoist subjects, resided in Jun-chou, that is, in Mao Shan country. He was said to have lacked enthusiasm for both religions.[8]

Ma Tai (fl. 853) was a poor boy who rose to be an important administrator and a much admired poet. Many of his poems treat Taoist themes.[9]

Yü Hsüan-chi (ca. 844–ca. 871), a courtesan, the friend of many distinguished men, finally became a Taoist priestess. She was a proud woman who considered herself the equal of any man. She was executed for killing a maidservant.[10]

Lu Kuei-meng (?–ca. 881) was an eccentric book collector and boatman who lived an austere life along the lower Yangtze, especially around the Grand Lake (T'ai Hu) and Mao Shan. He was a familiar of priests and hermits, at home among sacred cranes and at midnight stellar rituals, and a sincere student of the scriptures of Highest Clarity.[11]

P'i Jih-hsiu (?–ca. 881), the friend of holy men at Mao

Shan, and companion of Lu Kuei-meng, wrote many excellent poems about them. He is said to have been haughty and boastful, and was apparently a winebibber. He served the usurper Huang Ch'ao for a period, but in the end suffered death at his hands.[12]

Tu Kuang-t'ing (850–933), an ornament of the court of Wang Chien in Shu, was an ordained priest, a composer of ritual texts and poems about cruises among the stars, and a Taoist hagiographer of importance. His accounts of the careers of goddesses and divine princesses, full of the stuff of dreams and other worlds, are intended as testimony to the truth of the faith. Differently considered, these tales of the mysterious, the exotic, and the supernatural were characteristic of the popular genre of wonder tales which flourished so wonderfully in the late T'ang period.[13]

The light Coquettes in *Sylphs* aloft repair,
And sport and flutter in the Fields of Air.

ALEXANDER POPE
The Rape of the Lock

Poetic Forms with Taoist Content

SOME TRADITIONAL SONG-STYLES—named from their tunes, now unfortunately lost, each with its conventional scenario—lent themselves readily to Taoist treatment. Some, apparently, were devised only for that purpose. Such Taoist verse-fables are particularly noticeable among the "cantos" (*tz'u*) of the ninth and tenth centuries preserved in the classical anthology *Hua chien chi*. Among these song-forms are "Celestial Sylphling" (*T'ien hsien*

11

tzu), "The Transcendent Who Presides over the Kiang"
(*Lin chiang hsien*), "Autumn in the Osmanthus Basilica"
(*Kuei tien ch'iu*), "The Return of Esquire Juan" (*Juan lang
kuei*), "As in a Dream" (*Ju meng ling*), "Complaint of the
Ostracized Transcendent" (*Che hsien yüan*), and "Spirit of
the Ho Waterway" (*Ho tu shen*). Extant examples of verse-
fables in the form "Spirit of the Ho Waterway" are suffused
with a haunting supernatural atmosphere, but other forms
in this list seem to use Taoist imagery more for metaphor-
ical or symbolic purposes.

Two other song-forms that also belong in this group
have been the subject of my own special attention. Both are
richly invested with religious content and tone. One has
the title "The Female Capelines" (*Nü kuan tzu*), and its
scenario is always acted out by female Taoist neophytes
and priestesses whose identities are blended with those of
the high deities whose ranks they expect to join.[14] The
other tune is named "One Bit of Cloud at Shamanka
Mountain" (*Wu shan i tuan yün*). It evolved out of the old
"Music Archive" (*Yüeh fu*) song "Shamanka Mountain Is
High" (*Wu shan kao*), which in turn derives from features
of the long poems attributed to Sung Yü, *Kao T'ang fu* and
Shen nü fu. To the *Wu shan kao* style, dominated by the
evanescent figure of the Divine Woman lurking in the
mountain mists, writers of the Six Dynasties period added
the melancholy howling of the ape who embodies the ghost
of her long-dead royal lover. These same writers also began
to use the word "transcendent" (*hsien*), in the sense of
"lifted above the moils of this world," as a linguistic token
of a Taoist interpretation of the poems. Then, during the
T'ang period, the romantic presence of the poet-pilgrim—a
visitor to the shrine of the Divine Woman at the foot of her

mountain, rapt by dreams and visions, bewildered by phantoms and illusions—was added.[15] Cantos of the *Wu shan i tuan yün* variety are sometimes quite profane— secular retellings of the old "deserted lover" theme. But sometimes they reveal the haunting goddess and the haunted poet-pilgrim. Sometimes they provide a stage for a Taoist adept or even a vistor from the realm of the stars.

Two poets who composed cantos in this form have attracted my attention. They are Li Hsün (fl. 896), a Szech-wanese of Persian ancestry, author of the "Basic Herbal of Overseas Drugs" (*Hai yao pen ts'ao*),[16] and Ou-yang Chiung (896–971), also a luminary of the court of the king-dom of Shu, who is usually remembered for his preface to the *Hua chien chi.*[17] Both are known for their cantos in the form "A Southern Village" (*Nan hsiang tzu*), full of tropi-cal exoticism: complaisant Southern beauties in rose-pink garments, hibiscus, elephants, banana groves, pearl divers, and the like.[18] But both also wrote cantos on Taoist themes in the form *Wu shan i tuan yün.*[19]

Another poetic theme of respectable antiquity is embo-died in the religious chant called "Pacing the Void" (*Pu hsü [tz'u]*), examples of which survive from early Taoist liturgy and are sung in modern Taoist rites on Taiwan. Variations were composed by a number of T'ang poets, notably by Wei Ch'ü-mou and by Wu Yün, both men-tioned above.[20]

Finally we come to another "Music Archive" model, "Saunters in Sylphdom" (*Yu hsien*), whose treatment by Ts'ao T'ang is the subject of this study. The scenario is rooted in old poetic versions of shamanistic soul voyages, in particular the versions in the *Ch'u tz'u.* The standard medieval scenarios emerged at the end of the Han period with the compositions of Ts'ao Chih, Kuo P'u, and others, ultimately to be surpassed by the miraculous adaptations of this topos to the very different "Pacing the Void" scenario by Wu Yün. Despite its venerable history, the subject seems not to have attracted much professional attention, nor has much *Yu hsien* poetry been translated.

Some of the old sources of imagery exploited by Ts'ao T'ang have already been mentioned: *Lao tzu*, *Chuang tzu*, the *Ch'u tz'u*, and the rhapsodies of Sung Yü. To these must be added tales of wonders and marvels handed down from antiquity and early medieval times. The earliest of these at any rate were far from being merely imaginative fiction. Rather their writers "expressed the uncritical zeal of collectors of evidence for the truth of miracles, generating corresponding awe in their readers. These had their own simpler predecessors in accounts of otherwordly personages and places on the undisciplined fringes of civilization—such books as the *Mu t'ien tzu chuan* and the *Shan hai ching*. For them the world of spirits was a foreign world which occasionally intersected the familiar world. Few men doubted that the burning stars housed powerful spirits, or that trolls lurked in the fir forests, or that the kingdom of Ta Ch'in was inhabited by demigods."[21] Other collections of marvels of the post-Han period which undoubtedly inspired passages of Ts'ao T'ang's writings were the *Lieh hsien chuan*, *Shen hsien chuan*, *Han Wu ti nei chuan*, *Sou shen chi*, *Shih i chi*, *Yu ming lu*, and *Hai nei shih chou chi*. In addition to these there was the truly Taoist language of the *Chen kao*, the *Huang t'ing ching*, and other basic scriptures of the Mao Shan tradition.

To the above fertilizers of the field of diction must be added the esoteric language of alchemy. Necessarily the wonderful operations of that art (whose chief objective was

to compress and accelerate natural process), the consti-
tuents that went into them, and their final products, were
described and referred to by a special vocabulary. In effect,
this is the language of metaphor, which is also congenial to
poetry. Accordingly, it is not surprising that Ts'ao T'ang
has employed that language freely. Its scope ranges from
such simple substitutions, hallowed by antiquity, as "ti-
ger" for "lead," and "dragon" for "quicksilver," to truly
cabalistic phraseology, sometimes impossible to penetrate.
But occasionally the poet refers to chemical reagents quite
plainly, although, as is common with poets, with subtle
aims not obvious on a first reading. With this in mind, consider a sample of his work:

> Twenty years by a sanded torrent at a stony grotto;
> The sun, ferrying towards daylight, comes by night to the
>   Levee of Heaven.
> The white alum is evaporated in a mist, the quicksilver has
>   cooled;
> He is not aware that a small dragon lies asleep under his bed.
>   (83)[22]

This quatrain shows us a Taoist adept who labors in a limestone cavern by a mountain stream. He has spent the hours
of darkness carrying out an alchemical exercise, an analogue of the polar ritual of Highest Clarity, both of them
staged between midnight and dawn. Now the sun, like a
grandee, has been making the obligatory nocturnal journey
from his private house to be in place for the opening of the
cosmic court at daybreak. But the initiate, exhausted, lies
unaware that his astral chemistry has worked. A dragon,
the celestial counterpart of mercury and embryonic harbin-
ger of eternal life, has come into being in his private
chamber.

the blaze of uncreated light ...
Whose pure effulgence, radiant to excess,
No colours can describe, or words express.

SAMUEL BOYSE,
"Deity"

Terminology

THE READER WILL FIND in this study a number of uncommon words and strange expressions. Each of these is intended to convey simultaneously a reasonably exact notion of the sense of the Chinese original and of the atmosphere or tone its presence adds to the passage in which it appears. These expressions fall neatly into definable categories.

COSMOLOGY AND COSMOGRAPHY

The medieval Taoists were generally much concerned with realms (or states of being without particular location) beyond, or not related to, the several "skies" and "heavens"—even beyond the Great Enveloping Heaven (*ta lo t'ien*) that encloses the exalted heaven of Jade Clarity (*Yü Ch'ing*) where the sovereign of the universe holds court. These remoter parts of the universe frequently had the word "Grand" or "Greatest" or "Supreme" (*t'ai*) as the first element of their names. An example is Grand Homogeneity (*t'ai hun*), a locus, possibly a sphere, of undifferentiated protosubstance, a remnant of the primordial world before distinguishable entities emerged. Another is Grand Nimbus (*t'ai meng*), a dark cosmic mist—in effect, plasma made visible. There are also Grand Vortex (*t'ai yüan*), a pool of pure *yin*, and Grand Hoard (*t'ai yün*), a reservoir of potential forms. There are many other cosmographical expressions of this kind, but also some with differently constructed names, such as Barren Nullity (*hsü wu*), another remnant of a long-superseded state of things which can hardly be said to exist since it cannot be placed in space or time. Another is Transmuting Motor (*hua chi*), the cosmic generator which activates the created world.

Such terms as these are actually more characteristic of the poems of Wu Yün, including those named "Saunters in Sylphdom," than they are of Ts'ao T'ang's work. For the former writer, their use evokes a sense of unfathomable abysses, permeated by inconceivable energies. But when Ts'ao T'ang employs them, much more sparingly, it is to give a spacious background to intimate vignettes.

In the following quatrain, for example, he introduces the common cosmological term Grand Void (*t'ai hsü*). This normally refers to an insubstantial aether which precipitates tenuous substances, such as clouds, lunar halos, auroral mists, and the like from the Primal Pneuma (*yüan ch'i*) out of which the cosmos congealed at the beginning of time.[23] But Ts'ao T'ang conveys hardly more by that phrase than a suggestion of the remote home of his lady protagonist: it authenticates her credentials, and validates her costume and vehicle:

> The Lady of Western Han comes down from the Grand Void;
> Nine Auroras for her skirt band—Five Clouds her palanquin.
>   She intends to show me the cyan script for my instruction:
> She unties the wallet at her sash—takes out the Immaculate
>   Writ. (27)

The Nine Auroras (*chiu hsia*) are the vitalizing *yang*-plasmas from all of the Nine Heavens (this is a favorite phrase in Ts'ao T'ang's writing), that is, all the heavens that exist. They and the Five Clouds, the clouds tinted with the full spectrum of cosmic hues, were actually generated by the Grand Void.

The story is roughly as follows: A celestial preceptress descends from the dynamic center of the cosmos, her vestments shimmering with the soft colors of dawn, her space-car lapped by magic vapors. It is her duty to reveal to the expectant adept a true guide to eternal life beyond the stars: she shows him the prototype of an earthly scripture, this one written in celestial blue.[24]

In presenting this divine teacher as a rosy phantom, clad in pink streamers and apricot filaments torn, as it were, from the ejecta of sunrise, Ts'ao T'ang has created an otherworldly atmosphere without lapsing into the formulae of liturgy or the abstractions of astronomy. From the language of cosmography he has thus created an enchantment. So it is also with the glittering gardens, the glowing gems, and the colorful animals that populate these verses.

But while much of the vocabulary of cosmology can be

translated adequately with ordinary English words, the diction of T'ang Taoist poetry, including that written by Ts'ao T'ang, reveals a preference for rich, prismatic language rather than the abstractions of science—or, for that matter, of ritual. To capture the real sense and tone of these notions it is necessary to use some rather uncommon English words (like "watchet"), or to use English words in a rather specialized and restricted way (as "phosphor"), or even to invent new words (like "marchmount"). The most common of these in Ts'ao T'ang's verses are explained below. (The explanations provided are in many cases quoted directly from my own earlier publications.)

THE DIVINE WORLD

Aurora (*hsia*): This word is always used in its primary sense of the pink flush of dawn, never the false dawns of the aurora borealis and aurora australis.

Counterpart (*hsiang*): "Celestial events are the 'counterparts' or 'simulacra' of terrestrial events, sky things have doppelgängers below, with which they are closely attuned."[25]

Marchmount (*yüeh*): This rendering is preferred to the more conventional "sacred mountain" partly because there are many sacred mountains in China that are not *yüeh*, and partly because this set of five peaks represent "the four extremities of the habitable world, the marches of man's proper domain, the limits of the ritual tour of the Son of Heaven. There was, of course, a fifth—a kind of axial mount in the center of the world."[26]

Numinous (*ling*): This is the quality of "a spiritual force or energy emanating from or potential in any object full of mana, even such a dull thing as a stone. It radiated abundantly from imperial tombs, from powerful drugs, from magical animals, and from haunted trees. The souls of dead men were also called *ling* 'numen; holy spirit.'"[27]

Phosphor (*ching*): "This is a word for sky-lights of exceptional luminosity, suggesting a divine signal of particular intensity, normally with auspicious overtones.... cf. 'phosphor' as 'lucifer,' the conspicuous star of morning." Phosphors have counterparts. The visible phosphors (such as the sun and the moon, called "the Two Phosphors") are the "external phosphors," "other identities of the material concentrations of spiritual energy in the microcosm, the 'internal phosphors' (*nei ching*) of the human body."[28]

Pneuma (*ch'i*): This word means "breath" conceived as pregnant with vitality. There are many kinds of "breath" throughout both the macrocosm and the microcosm. An example is "earth breaths" (*ti ch'i*), "energetic emanations of local soil topography—the active principles of what we now call biomes. The results of the activity of these pneumas were faunal, floral, mineral, and even cultural zones."[29] For example, the earth breath of the southern provinces determines that the local citrus fruit shall be a tangerine, rather than the thorny lime of the north. In metaphysical and cosmological contexts "pneuma" seems a more suitable translation of *ch'i* than "breath," being free from organic associations: in some ways it reminds one of Henri Bergson's *élan vital*.

Primal Pneuma (*yüan ch'i*): This is the original creative spirit which generated the cosmos, beginning with the separation of *yin* and *yang*, like the mitosis of a cosmic zygote. Sometimes it congeals into visible mists, hazes, and prismatic nebulosities; it is from these that the homes of the gods are formed. The Taoists believe that such eternal beings as Jade Women crystallized directly from the Primal Pneuma.[30]

TAOIST DIVINITIES

Transcendent (*hsien*): This is a member of a word-family which connotes such things as light-stepping, walking on air, going about with one's head in the clouds, carefree and buoyant. In mythology it was used of a class of beings also known as "plumed persons" (*yü jen*), represented pictorially in Han times with feathered arms, reminding us of the peris of Iran. (The name *pari* means "winged one", from *par* "feather; wing.") They look like crystalline children, eat no solid food, and fly through the air, sometimes riding on clouds and auras. In Taoism the condition of a *hsien* is somewhat more etherealized, suggesting, beyond merely the magic power of flight, escape from the passions, attachments, filth, and illusions of the mortal condition. I usually call these beings "transcendents," implying that they have the power to transcend earthly corruption, but sometimes I style them "sylphs" because of their resemblance to the delicate, airy elementals of western tradition. They are not "immortal," however, and must constantly renew their vital powers.

Realized [Person] (*chen [jen]*): This expression was in use before the rise of organized medieval Taoism, but only in a casual way. In Highest Clarity, or Mao Shan Taoism, it refers to fully developed persons who have attained a recognized place in the hierarchy of superbeings—a position higher than that occupied by the transcendents. They have attained their exalted status by virtue of an endowment of exceptional talents while in their mortal condition, by their application to rigorous disciplines leading to mastery of their inner selves, and by their complete understanding of the most arcane scriptures. In short, these transmuted humans are entirely unlike the disembodied ghosts of ordinary men, who roam the world disconsolately, or are held fast in glacial dungeons by the demoniac myrmidons of the dread King of the North. The epithet "realized" implies that they have fully realized their potentials as human beings, or, to put it another way, they have perfected themselves. Their new selves are as insusceptible to physiological inquiry as they are to corruption. They are no longer organic but share the properties of precious gems and metals. They are mineral entities—and often luminescent, like the "night-shining jade women" of scripture.[31] In the minds of visionaries and poets, they must have resembled a certain inhabitant of our own world:

> One would think that the body was adorned with a diadem of brilliant gems. The middle organs of the eyes shone with ultramarine blue, the lateral ones with a pearly sheen. Those towards the front of the lower surface of the body gave out a ruby-red light, while those behind were snow-white or pearly, except the median one, which was sky-blue. It was indeed a glorious spectacle.[32]

Unlike Professor Chun's deep-sea squid, however, realized persons dwell forever in the heaven or condition called Highest Clarity, above the upper levels of the realm of Grand Clarity (*T'ai Ch'ing*), which is inhabited by "transcendents." They are entitled to access to the receptions and levees at the high courts of those almost inconceivable creatures, the elemental powers and faceless dynamos who reside, and will reside forever, above them, in the shimmering world of Jade Clarity:

There are also celestial bodies, and bodies terrestrial: but the glory of the celestial is one, and the glory of the terrestrial is another.[33]

And:

For this corruptible must put on incorruption, and this mortal must put on immortality.[34]

Thearch (*ti*): In antiquity this title referred to the spirits of dead kings, some later euhemerized as sages and culture heroes. In the third century B.C. it was adopted as a title of the Son of Heaven, and this practice became routine. To the modern mind this usage seems ambiguous, but was not so to the ancient Chinese. The situation in the western world was long the same. To take only a few well-known parallels, Alexander the Great was a god; his successors in Asia and Africa, especially the Ptolemies, were gods. They held titles like Epiphanes "[god] made manifest," Soter "savior," and even Theos "god." The deification of Augustus Caesar and his successors is even more familiar.[35] In the Han state religion *ti* remained the proper title of the most powerful deities. Similarly it designated the most exalted gods of the Taoist pantheon, particularly those in Jade Clarity.

COLORS AND GEMS

Blue and red are polarized in Chinese poetry, and are represented by a great number of word-pairs, the basic dyad being "cinnabar-azurite" (*tan ch'ing*), the standard red and blue mineral pigments of the traditional Chinese palette. These have spawned numerous progeny, such as "gibbon's blood" (*hsing-hsing hsüeh*), the name of a scarlet dye, going with ultramarine (*se-se*), the pigment made by powdering lapis lazuli.[36] "Cyan" or "indigo" (*pi*) is the color of the depths of space, regularly contrasted with "auroral" (*hsia*), the rosy flush of dawn. For Ts'ao T'ang, red is the proper color of the simurghs (*luan*) that serve as mounts or draw the carriages of the deities. These are correctly ruddy, since they are incarnations (or emanations) of the great Red Bird who presides over the South. Similarly, the dragons that wing through "Saunters in Sylphdom" are rightly blue, since the Blue (or Green) Dragon represents the cosmic aspects of the East, as well as vernal renewal and life, and it can often be recognized as the conveyance of Blue Lad, Lord of the East. Here are a few more color terms that may be obscure.

Rose-gold (*chiang*): "Originally this was the name of a pigment made by mixing a red substance with yellow gambodge—in short, it corresponded to some hue between 'orange' and 'scarlet.' But the word has also been defined in Chinese as 'like the color of the emerging sun.' This flame-like color appears repeatedly both in Taoist poetry and in the canonical scriptures."[37]

Watchet (*ts'ang*): This is "the color of the iron-gray or blue-gray sea, for which I like the old word 'watchet.'"[38] Consider the matched pair from an English poet, "In sober watchet, umber sad."[39]

Mystic (*hsüan*): This word is apparently cognate to *hsün* "fumes," hence "murky" and the unsettling obscurity of mist-shrouded things; by extension, that which is shrouded from vulgar view—arcane, etc.

In descriptions of divine mansions and gardens, the enigmatic names of forgotten gems serve to suggest not only their unearthly nature but their glittering or adamantine lusters. Most common of these are the following:

Rose-gem (*ch'iung*): This is "an archaic gem name, whose precise reference was lost by medieval times. A number of glosses and contexts indicate that before Han it was a semiprecious red stone, possibly an old name for carnelian."[40] Some medieval writers use it for a perfectly white gem, the material of the fruits and flowers of paradise. "Rose-gem" was suggested as a translation for *ch'iung* by rhodonite, a pink carbonate of manganese.

Azure-gem (*yao*): In pre-Han times this word was used of "ornamental stone insets in ritual vessels; it may have been turquoise or malachite, or both. A blue-green association was retained after Han, when the specific identity of the mineral had been forgotten.... The persistence of the word as a handsome epithet of waters and grasses suggests that, for many writers at least, this association had not been forgotten even in T'ang times.... Perhaps our rather obsolete gem name 'smaragd' could be used to translate it."[41] ("Carbuncle and smaragd" would be more suitable for fairy towers made of these two stones than would the dubious precision of "garnet and turquoise.") I have adopted the translation "azure-gem" by association with the names of the blue minerals lapis lazuli and azurite.

Translations

TO EXPLAIN MY VIEWS on the translation of
Chinese poetry, I will simply restate what I have said elsewhere:

> I have little automatic reverence of "masterpieces," and regard
> my translations as nothing more than aspects of explication—
> instruments which may help wise men to detect masterpieces.
> I am certainly not trying to write English poetry—to make
> pleasing constructs in lieu of hidden Chinese originals—a task
> for which I am ill suited. In particular I have tried to avoid
> dressing medieval Chinese verse in twentieth-century Amer-

ican garb.... I regard almost all approved translations of T'ang poetry as malignant growths. They tell us approximately as much about the real meaning and character of T'ang poems as the works of Winckelmann and Canova tell us about the art of ancient Hellas—probably much less. How dreary Tu Fu and Li Po appear in the drab robes laid over them by contemporary taste.... In the end, the aim of my stolid prose renderings is the subversion of most sinological gospel.[42]

Nevertheless, I obviously translate poetry. My purpose is to hold up the mirror to the world of Ts'ao T'ang's imagination, and to the unique medieval culture that nurtured it. Therefore, I believe that it is my responsibility to corrupt his strange and wonderful originals as little as possible. I must repress my sense of the "poetic" and "appropriate," and strive only to provide reliable information about the words and combinations of words—the metaphors and other images—that constitute the fabric of his linguistic artifacts. Translation may prove useful in reflecting some facets of the dazzling creations that survive from another era, another civilization, another person. But every work of art is self-contained and unique: no amount of information about it can evoke anything better than a dark and deformed image of the original. The real poem exists only in the literary language of ninth-century China.

Part One

TS'AO T'ANG AND
HIS ELYSIAN ENCOUNTERS

Through her fine limbs the mimic lightnings
    dart,
And flames innocuous eddy round her heart;
O'er her fair brow the kindling lustres glare,
Blue rays diverging from the bristling hair;
While some fond Youth the kiss eternal sips.
And soft fires issue from their meeting lips.

ERASMUS DARWIN
The Economy of Vegetation, I, 351-356

      Ts'AO T'ANG, agnomen Yao-pin, was born
in the northern part of what is now Kwangsi, either in
Kuei-chou or in Liu-chou.[1] In that period both were fron-
tier towns buried in a seemingly endless monsoon forest.
His birth and death dates are unknown, but he was active
in the 860s and 870s. He was an intimate of the more
famous writer Lo Yin, who was in his thirties and forties
during those decades. We may reasonably assume that
Ts'ao T'ang belonged to the same generation.

Little is known of his life. In his youth he was a devoted Taoist,[2] and one late source states that he was a priest.[3] However, he aspired to civil rank, and in about mid-century he was selected to try for the degree of "Advanced Gentleman" (*chin shih*) at the capital. Evidently he failed in this, for during the 860s he was obliged to be content with secretarial posts at the headquarters of provincial warlords.[4]

Various fantastic accounts of the poet's death survive, all of them sharing the theme of a premonitory visit by one or more celestial women. One of these tales tells that when the poet lay ill in a Buddhist monastery, the K'ai Yüan Szu at Hsin-chou in what is now Kiangsi, the monks saw two women dressed in blue (evidently jade women) approach. The brethren thought that these must be the two divine women of Mount T'ien T'ai who had entertained the young gentlemen Liu Ch'en and Juan Chao in their sanctuary of flowering peaches.[5] They hastened to the poet's chamber and found him dead. The phantoms had vanished.[6]

Few of Ts'ao T'ang's writings survive, and very little is known about what has vanished. He is reputed to have written a prose work in one scroll entitled "The Mysterious Archive of the Purple Orb" (*Tzu chu hsüan fu*),[7] certainly a Taoist treatise. Other than this, we know virtually nothing. As for his verses, the "Complete T'ang Poetry" (*Ch'üan T'ang shih*) preserves ninety-eight of his Little Saunters in Sylphdom (*Hsiao yu hsien shih*),[8] some of which are the object of this study.[9] He is said to have composed a set of fifty Greater Saunters in Sylphdom (*Ta yu hsien shih*), but none of these has survived under that name.[10] The remainder of his poems is gathered in the first of the two sections which constitute the extant corpus in the *Chüan T'ang shih*. Of these, the majority treat Taoist themes, in much the same manner as the Saunters in Sylphdom. One reports the visit of the Royal Mother of the West to Han Wu Ti, and another describes the banquet that monarch prepared for her in his palace. The former is, characteristically, a rich vision of blue birds and shining simurghs, of moon dew and the sound of bells, of tree shadows and the blowing of panpipes, while the latter reveals the Altar of the Grand Monad (*T'ai i t'an*), invested with an atmosphere of powerful magic. It is set under a clear night sky: all is cold, white, clear, and delicate—uncontaminated with tokens of mortal corruption. There are a number of other poems on the subject of encounters between a mortal and a divinity—subjects which he also treats in his "Saunters." We find the familiar figures of the two youths Liu Ch'en and Juan Chao and the two fairy maidens with whom they consorted at Mount T'ien T'ai. In a similar vein he recounts the story of the Weaving Woman and her cow-tending lover on the banks of the Sky River, our Milky Way. He presents the mysterious divinity Wang Yüan, wearing a sorcerer's robe covered with medallions showing "the starry dipper in little skies," about to invite the bird-footed goddess Miss Hemp to a party. He describes a feast given by the Tranquil Son of Heaven (*Mu t'ien tzu*) in honor of the Royal Mother of the West; the king is strangely, but correctly, placed in an Eden out in the eastern ocean, and the language is rich in appropriate tokens—auroral colors, dark blue flowers, the rising sun, rainbows, and gemmy sands. He also tells how Hsiao Shih, the incomparable player of the syrinx, ascended the sky with the maiden Lung-yü.

Apart from such haunted liaisons and mystical banquets, Ts'ao T'ang treated many other supernatural and fairytale (if that is not too skeptical a term) themes like Han Wu Ti's lament for his beloved Lady Li; the dangerous forests on the slopes of Mount Lo-fou, with elephants and rhinos infesting the region where Ko Hung cooked his elixirs; the otherworldly beauty of the hermitages and grottos of Mount Heng in the south; eerie phosphorescence (*yin huo*) seen under a white-damask moon, with the sound of flutes; dead soldiers lying in the frosty beech forests of the hateful northlands; a shining sword pulsating with magic power. A few poems allude to events in his own life: he visits the mountain over a grotto heaven in Chekiang, where strange rocks provide roosts for cranes; late in life, his hair turning gray, he entertains gloomy thoughts of a country hermitage; he reports a great Taoist ceremony on behalf of the ruling family; he expresses satisfaction with his courtyard where he has recently planted a pair of pines.

Despite the recurrence of a limited number of plots, scenarios, stage settings, and actors throughout the Ts'ao T'ang corpus, their realizations are richly varied, and the poet has created a large number of highly distinctive subplots and recurrent motifs. Each of these, with its attendant atmospheric effects, might form the subject of a special study. Here are just a few:

The hierarchy of Jade Women

The hieratic significance of high fashion among the gods and illuminati

Alchemy as a mode of imaging the external world

The diet of Taoist overlords: mineral ambrosias and crystalline nectars

Astral gardens as sites for seduction

And so on, with increasing subtlety of definition, almost ad infinitum. I shall allude to only a few of these, and some of them only lightly, as I introduce Ts'ao T'ang's poetic work with a study of those stanzas among the "Saunters in Sylphdom" which deal with the theme of the clouded and evanescent sea-isles—just one of the arenas in which his tantalizing and equivocal tableaux are staged. It may not be amiss, however, to admit here some other thematic material as particularly relevant to a study of the larger topic of the Elysian Isles, sketching some of the persons, places, situations, and concepts that constitute the linguistic molecules of Ts'ao T'ang's jeweled pleasure domes, and their scenes of pageantry, pleasure, folly, and regret.

Many of his vignettes are set in gardens—or approximations of gardens: perhaps the environs of a flowering tree; the parklands surrounding a celestial palace; a botanical garden full of choice medicinal growths; an island in the sea. But the poet reveals only one corner of the garden. It is as if he had woven a rich and intricate tapestry, and then destroyed all but a fragment, from which the reader must infer the design of the whole.

In some sense these enigmatic parvises are all sacred precincts and at the same time trysting places. The secrets shared there partake both of the profane and of the divine. All are the equivalents of Eden, or of Elysium, or of the *hortus conclusus*—the secret rose-garden of the queen of heaven.[11]

The couple who anticipate or achieve a mystic union there may be stellated humans, or truly eternal beings, personifications of alchemical reagents, representing the dispersing *yang* and the conserving *yin*, partly fleshed out. They are Adam and Eve—or merely marionettes. In any case, they represent universal forces whose interaction accounts for all of Creation: "l'amor che move il sole e l'altre stelle."[12]

But the identities of the participants in these pretty masquerades are fluid. Even when appearing and behaving most human, they are in fact phosphorescent star-kings and fluorescent goddesses. For a true adept, the courtier and his lady are both phantoms and illusions, masks adopted for the moment as means of identification. If properly prepared, he would see, behind the pretty face, the elaborate coiffure, and the richly embroidered gown, an inorganic being, animated by crystalline ducts and hyaline glands. The Jade Woman of the Cinnabar Aurora of the Highest Mysteries of the Greatest Mystery (*T'ai hsüan shang hsüan tan hsia yü nü*), an entity of great power, conjured to appear before the trained initiate poised in the disk of the moon, reveals herself to him dressed in a skirt and stole of vermilion damask, with a jaunty purple cap on her head.[13]

It is in their phenomenal aspects that Ts'ao T'ang also presents his actors to his readers. Their noumenal character must be guessed by the members of his audience, relying on their own familiarity with the standard icons, as well as on the skill of Ts'ao T'ang's writing. But ultimate things are also present in the poems: the bell that sounds from its painted tower sounds the knell of a whole generation of men and of gods; the warm wind from P'eng-lai assures the transcendents another three thousand years of life. On the surface, the young heroes who march through these stanzas are, except for their formal attributes and blazonry, very much alike. They figure as examples of careless youth, unaware of mortality, preoccupied with their fugitive impulses, ignorant of their own folly. Their soul-mates are yearning girls, usually dissatisfied with their responsibilities or secluded situations, expectant of a divine love. There are a few exceptions: some great goddesses, such as the Royal Mother of the West, occupy dominant positions. They may occasionally sigh after a departing gentleman, but are not likely to languish for very long.

On the whole the masculine figures, even though they are in some ways as interchangeable as the busbied young gentlemen of a regiment of hussars, stand out in bolder relief than their charming companions, who, despite such elegant but really anonymous titles as Golden Consort, Chosen Woman, and Transcendent Child, seem little more individualized than the soubrettes, grisettes, and midinettes of nineteenth-century West European literature.

The cast of characters who saunter into and out of these pantomimes, named or recognized, is rather long, but the chief performers can be enumerated as follows:

EARLY KINGS AND ARCHIMAGES

The Tranquil Son of Heaven (*Mu t'ien tzu*) is the title of a king said to have ruled over Chou in the tenth century B.C. He is reputed to have been a great traveler in foreign parts, an inspector of the marches. He climaxed his career by entertaining the Royal Mother of the West at a magnificent banquet. For Ts'ao T'ang he is a celestial prince, fully her equal, and her spiritual lover.[14]

The Martial Thearch of Han (*Han wu ti*) is another historical figure who acquired a new personality by legendary transformation. Offered the opportunity to achieve immortality from the hands of the Royal Mother of the West, he proved wanting in dedication to higher truth, and died like any other mortal.[15]

Tung-fang Shuo was a wit and jesting adviser to the Martial Thearch.[16] In legend he acquired magical powers and endless youth. He, too, met the Royal Mother, and in the end was stellated as the planet Jupiter or, according to a different tradition, as Venus.[17]

An-ch'i Sheng was a wonder-worker reputed to have lived in the days of the Inaugural Resplendent Thearch of Ch'in (*Ch'in shih huang ti*). He was associated with the holy isle P'eng-lai, and knew the art of lengthening life with miraculous jujubes.[18]

MYTHICAL HEROES

Wang Tzu-chin, also styled Wang Tzu-ch'iao or simply Wang Ch'iao,[19] was reputed to have been Grand Heir (*t'ai tzu*) to the Numinous King of Chou (*Chou ling wang*) in the sixth century B.C. He excelled at playing the reed-organ, and had an intimate acquaintance with sacred cranes. He ultimately attained transcendence, and the rank of Supervisor of Destinies in a secret palace at Mount T'ien T'ai.[20]

Hsiao Shih is said to have been a man of the state of Ch'in in the seventh century B.C. He was another magical musician, a master of the syrinx (*hsiao*), which gave him power over divine birds, like Wang Tzu-chin and Orpheus. He had a special affinity with the phoenix, and after he had married a princess both were transformed into phoenixes.[21]

Liu Ch'en and **Juan Chao** are the quintessential young Percivals, although the object of their quest was nothing so specific as a grail, and they were not averse to spiritual unions with charming oreads. Their story is set in the year 62 A.D., when they went into the remote parts of Mount T'ien T'ai in search of medicinal plants. They lost their way and wandered without food. At the cost of much effort they found a peach tree in full fruit on the summit of a precipice. They ate of the fruit and were immediately hale. They were further nourished by magic cakes that floated out from a mysterious grotto. Supposing this to be a route to the world of men, they pursued the stream, which led them to a pleasant place. There they found two young women, who entertained them in a richly appointed house. Eventually infatuation was consummated in love. But with the advent of the following spring, the two youths felt homesick and were allowed to depart. They found the world they knew completely gone: seven human generations had passed. In the year 383 they went off again, and were never heard from further.[22] These spiritual twins are popular figures in T'ang poetry as images of the perfect lover. If unnamed, their presence can often be detected by the sight of a swallet, a stream emerging from a grotto, especially if there are peach blossoms on it. In "Taoist" poetry, emphasis is put on the great difference between the slow passage of time in the hidden world beyond the grotto as compared with the rush towards decay and death in the mortal world.[23]

TAOIST DIVINITIES

Mao Chung, is the third of the eponymous trio of brothers for whom Mao Shan Taoism is named, all of whom, as is fitting, occupy exalted positions in the hierarchy of Highest Clarity. He is an inspector of the credentials of the dead, rejoicing in the title of Lesser Lord Mao, Conservator of Destinies for the Three Magistrates (*San kuan pao* *ming hsiao Mao chün*).[24] It is a little surprising to see him so approachable in Ts'ao T'ang's setting.[25]

Blue Lad (*Ch'ing T'ung*) threads his often enigmatic way through many of the scenes that follow. He is King of the Elysian Isles. Much remains to be said of him.

NYMPHS AND GODDESSES

Few of these exalted ladies have traceable careers in Chinese myth and legend, the great exception being Hsi Wang Mu, the Royal Mother of the West, whose mutations, attributes, and associations have been widely studied.[26] Briefly, in Taoist literature she is Queen of the West, of the world axis, of the ladder to heaven. She is infinitely beautiful, desirable, and elusive. She is the companion and preceptress of mighty kings and exalted deities. In Ts'ao T'ang's quatrains she is regularly paired with Blue Lad, but he is also her antithesis—her mirror image in the East. They are brother and sister, husband and wife, totally worthy of each other, like the perfect but incestuous sovereigns of Egypt. She is the most powerful of oreads, who can look upon the stupefying countenance of the Lord of the Universe with tranquility—or dally in her jeweled garden with young aspirants to celestial glory. There is none like her.

Other female figures in Ts'ao T'ang's often ambiguous pairings are, for the most part, her talented ladies-in-waiting, such as Tung Shuang-ch'eng, a virtuoso performer on the reed-organ, and the Lady of the Highest Prime (*Shang Yüan fu-jen*), whose talent was to perform on the *ao* of Cloudy Forest, evidently a kind of lithophone.[27] Otherwise, the celestial ladies of these poems are poorly characterized, and identified only by such non-distinctive labels as Select Woman (*ts'ai nü*), Jade Woman (*Yü nü*),

Attendant Woman (*shih nü*), and Transcendent Child (*hsien tzu*). To balance the score somewhat, it is Ts'ao T'ang's style to allude even to important "males" in the most discreet and indirect way—the flutter of a blue sleeve, the sound of a particular woodwind—leaving it to the reader to supply the appropriate name or title.

Secret trysts, with their attendant anticipations and inevitable separations, are highly characteristic of the Saunters in Sylphdom. They are regularly set in a context of larger social gatherings, which sometimes appear to be the main theme of the quatrain, but are most often only part of the scenery, hardly as prominent as the corps de ballet in the presence of the prima donna of a grand opera. Indeed, it is very characteristic of these "transcendent" or "realized" persons to socialize constantly, even when they may have been convened for some more serious purpose: they spend more time in the garden or at the refreshment table than listening to the speaker of the day, just as it is in our times and climes. They seem to be perpetually winging back and forth between palaces and pleasaunces, listening to concerts in well-appointed flower gardens, and flirting behind the hedges.

The protagonists, male or female, regularly find themselves detached from the general merriment, searching, often hopelessly, for a particular person. Inextricably linked with this traditional search for the beloved one is the motif of parting, separation, and loss, which is hardly distinguishable from the uncertain mood of expectation and longing. At the heart of these dreamlike episodes is the secret enclosure—the lonely place of awakening love and springtime, which is also the site of fading love and falling leaves.

Very commonly the secret place of assignation is a grotto, figured as a halfway house, a limbo, a place of transition, of initiation, of realization, or, as it may be, of rejection. It is a place of seclusion—a womb or sanctum or grave—where all things are possible, including the birth of divine love or rebirth into a new world and life in a new cosmos. Here death is symbolic: it may mean the interval between the old life and the new, or it may mean the loss of divine aspirations and the consequent return to the mortal world and its inevitable conclusion. This allegory is not confined to the poems of Ts'ao T'ang. It appears elsewhere in T'ang poetry, notably in the *tz'u*-form called *Nü kuan tzu*.[28] In these haunted cantos the twilight zone just inside the mouth of the grotto is more often a place of frustration and loss of hope than it is of meeting and fulfillment, as the following examples show.

A priestess expects the arrival of a divine lover: "In flowered grotto she loathes his late arrival." Or again, "Inside the grotto: knotted with misery, in vain." Finally: "Gloomily heard in grotto-heaven: the spaced-out chimes.... In what place now are Liu and Juan? Messages from them are cut off."

For Ts'ao T'ang, the shadowy adit or aven[29] that leads to the underworld is typically a boundary between the sacred and the profane worlds. In the following specimen the maiden stands just inside the grotto, peering out into the world of men. In this she is unlike the female neophytes of the Capeline Cantos who look hopefully into the shadowy depths from the world of light. Accordingly, the sought-for Galahad is, in Ts'ao T'ang's treatment, out among mortals—and indeed he is no other than our romantic friend Liu Ch'en, who had the bad judgment to leave his fairy lover in the peach blossom grotto of Mount T'ien T'ai:

She comes stealthily to the mouth of the grotto in search of
Master Liu;
Stepping slowly, she lifts her jade-threaded skirt lightly in
both hands.
Delicately she snaps off a peach blossom and sends it away on
the flowing water:
But there are no words now—no speech, as she leans against a
red-tinted cloud. (26)

The young goddess is shown sending a love token and a
reminder of an old liaison—but the peach blossom is also
an invitation to another and more perfect hierogamy.

The theme of the outward flowing water that carries a
message to the unconfined and enticing outer world is a
common one in T'ang poetry. It is found also in completely secular contexts, as when a lonely inmate of the palace
commits a message written on a leaf out through the drains,
dreaming that it will be found by a desirable youth[30]—like
the letter dropped from a prison window, or the note
penned on a desert island and entrusted to the waves. The
choice of a peach flower is significant in several ways. It is
the traditional link between the fairy women and the lost
youths at T'ien T'ai, and it is also associated with the Royal
Mother of the West in her role of goddess of love and fertility. It suggests awakening romance, tremulous initiation,
and the promise of total fulfillment. Peach blossoms are
also associated with the seamount P'eng-lai. Taoist priests
and chasmophilous[31] recluses planted peach trees at the
mouths of mysterious grottoes, near their altars to the star-
gods.[32]

The poem shares another motif with the Capeline
Cantos—and with other Taoist love poetry: the divine
maiden's loss of speech. In the Cantos that theme is played

on in a multitude of ways: reduced speech, muted speech, no speech at all, presumably to create an atmosphere of the world of spirits who, if they speak at all, whisper mysterious syllables, or warble sweetly, like white-winged angels.[33] Here one of the twin goddesses of T'ien T'ai, having transmitted her thoughts in the language of flowers, has no need of verbal communication. She waits, faint with expectancy, leaning on a magically congealed cloud (clouds regularly represent numinous presences within a grotto) flushed with the evidence of eternal life.

But often, very often, such expectations as these are doomed to frustration, as much those of royal lovers and heavenly queens as those of girlish acolytes. The advent of a sacred being cannot be commanded, nor its attention counted on, nor its concern expected with confidence.[34] All true epiphanies and all divine gifts are necessarily spontaneous. This is why these poems are sprinkled with allusions to broken engagements, missing messages, and every sort of disappointment.

As for the magic flowers, whether those of the peach, the pear, or the apricot, they represent transition—transition in space or in time, for better or for worse: death and rebirth, the cycle of seasons, the relativity of mortal dimensions. The flowers that ornament the secular poetry of T'ang are conspicuously absent from Taoist poetry: we find no roses, no chrysanthemums, no peonies, no lotuses in the latter. The themes of frailty, decay, senescence, even among the gods—barely concealed by a thin veil of frivolity and lightheartedness—are characteristic of Ts'ao T'ang's writing. In this he differs markedly from Wu Yün, whose poems on Pacing the Void and on Saunters in Sylphdom are full of exuberant confidence. For him it is "Paradise Regained"—Ts'ao T'ang shows paradise perpetually fading on the horizon.

Time, as people say, is of the essence. In other poetry the swift passage of the hours, measuring off the limits of life, is often symbolized by the rising and setting of the sun, the moon, or the stars, marking the days, months, and years respectively.[35] In Ts'ao T'ang's quatrains it is usually the sweet-smelling flowers shaken loose and tattered by the chill winds from the spectral northern lands that represent corruption and dissolution. Here is an example.

> The Gentleman-Technician's volant coach halts by the auroral flush in the deep blue;
> The wine is cold, the wind is chilly, the moon begins to slant down.
> He does not know who is singing "The Song for the Return of Spring"—
> But all are fallen, every one of the white kudzu flowers at river's head. (63)

This is the tale: A magician who has learned the art of space travel stops his elegant car under the remotest part of the eastern sky. He finds the festivities of spring long concluded, and sees tokens of disenchantment and decay everywhere: it is the onset of the cosmic autumn. He hears a voice chanting a spell for the rebirth of the world and the beginning of a new time cycle. The last of the spirit-flowers—kudzu blossoms are usually pink, but white suggests death—fall into the divine garden.[36]

Such is the ground bass (*basso ostinato*) of Ts'ao T'ang's Taoist fantasies, but the high counterpoint is provided by his witty courtly masques, richly and carefully furnished, and often glossed with a light, playful tone and refined glamor—the hallmarks of ephemera.

Other *yu hsien* poets show us (in effect) happy children engaged in innocent play in paradise gardens, sometimes accompanied by tokens of domestic bliss, rather like the saints in Gustav Mahler's Fourth Symphony:

> Kein Musik ist ja nicht auf Erden
> die uns'rer verglichen kann werden.
> Elftausend Jungfrauen zu tanzen sich trauen!
> Sanct Ursula selbst dazu lacht!

Unlike these writers, Ts'ao T'ang introduces the denizens of heaven not as modest and unassuming saints, but as members of an elite class, comparable to an assemblage of high ecclesiastics and secular lords and ladies. Sometimes his verses remind us of Renaissance pleasantries about the amours of Mars and Venus, or the farcical antics of the Olympian gods in the works of Offenbach, such as *La Belle Hélène* and *Orphée aux enfers*. Underneath these enchanting visions, however, the drama of time and mutability is being played out. Behind even the smooth and shining faces of the deities lies a grinning skull. The message is monitory: "O Man, take heed!" This apparent ambiguity of tone suggests the "provisional playfulness" that has been detected in the poetry of Erasmus Darwin.[37] The term is meant to describe a kind of humorous disclaimer of serious intent or real commitment:

> ... like the eternal secrets of any mystery religion, which would neither be understood nor accepted by ordinary, complacent, small-minded men, these truths are concealed under a ludicrous, half-serious tone.... He believes, but he cannot believe seriously.[38]

Ts'ao T'ang, in his poems, is dealing with an inner-directed faith, aimed at personal salvation, strongly tinged with elitism. Possibly, after entering secular society, he still wished to believe in the Taoist cosmic order and the exalted place reserved in it for certain elect beings. The poems express, perhaps pathetically, the need for this lost confidence. He has reshaped the tenets of the faith in poetic episodes, and clothed them in a semihuman mythology. The result is an almost perversely incongruous mixture of high theology and courtly frivolity—his uncertainty is revealed as a kind of wry mockery. Unlike Offenbach, whose Olympians are fictitious comedians, Ts'ao T'ang deals with only partially demystified superbeings, still invested with real power and glory. His poetic visions make them real and accessible—but he seems not to doubt that somehow they exist, and have authority over life and death.

Part Two

PRINCIPALITIES OF
THE SEA

Far-gleaming o'er the town, transparent fanes
Rear their white towers, and wave their golden
    vanes;
Long lines of Lustres pour their trembling rays
And the bright vault returns the mingled blaze.

ERASMUS DARWIN
The Loves of the Plants, V, 323–326

P'eng-lai

FOR THE CHINESE of T'ang the mysterious
East was more complex than the mysterious West. The
westlands, beyond those known to Chinese soldiers and
caravaneers, were dominated by the towering image of
Mount K'un-lun. But the farthest eastern horizon, visible
only to Korean seafarers and visiting Japanese monks on
whom the Chinese landlubbers of the Middle Ages had to
depend for knowledge of those waters, was still far from
even more fabulous lands, closer to the birthplace of the
sun, the seats of powerful deities. There were two such

wonderlands. The closer was the floating island—or
islands—of P'eng-lai, the analogue of K'un-lun, and also of
Mount Lo-fou in southern Kwangtung. Half of Mount Lo-
fou had floated in from the sea long ago, to attach itself to
its landlocked twin, like the fragment of a tectonic plate
merging with a Mesozoic continent; some say that this
fragment was part of P'eng-lai itself.[1] And far beyond
P'eng-lai lay Fu-sang, the magnificent home of the lord of
the reborn sun.

P'eng-lai was a lower paradise, like the slopes of K'un-
lun, strewn with the delightful gardens of eternally happy
beings. Fu-sang was an inextinguishable powerhouse concealed behind a facade of divine splendor: we shall catch a
glimpse of it later.

The most ancient accounts of P'eng-lai are preserved in
the old histories that tell of the Ch'in empire and the early
Han. These accounts raised high hopes that the secrets of
everlasting life might be found over the eastern horizon.
The intermediary whose goodwill and assistance seemed
essential to the realization of this dream was the Prior Born
An-ch'i, reputed to be a dealer in drugs along the eastern
coast who had achieved immortality on that distant island.
To worthy mortals he might offer one of the huge, miraculous jujubes that seem to have been necessary if not sufficient to attain that wonderful goal.[2] He has frequently
been remembered in poetry and popular tales,[3] and was not
overlooked by Ts'ao T'ang. Like his successor, Blue Lad,
the divine playboy of the East, he is represented in these
verses as the idol and ideal beau of celestial soubrettes:

> The servant girl raises a flagon of jade wine in her own hands;
> The whole flagon is drained of wine as she presses it on An-
> ch'i.

> She parted from him carelessly three thousand years ago—
> But has long remembered the time when they shared his
>   jujubes on the river margin. (56)

This love-smitten housemaid is doubtless one of the jade
lasses attendant upon the Royal Mother of the West at
K'un-lun, a place not associated with Master An-ch'i in
antiquity. With the passage of three thousand years a cosmic epoch has been concluded, and a new one begins. She
regrets her indifference to the great wonder-worker when
he last came to visit her mistress. (More remains to be said
about the flowery clock of eternity and the periodic drying
up of the sea, which mark these epochs.)

The early Han sources give only a simple, rather juvenile
image of the homeland of Lord An-ch'i. They agree that it
is in the Eastern Sea—indeed, not too far from the lands of
men—but few reach it, since relentless storms drive all
ships away from its shores.[4] In January of 103 B.C., in rites
ancillary to those performed in honor of the great earth
deity, the Martial Thearch of Han worshiped far P'eng-lai
from the eastern verge of his empire.[5]

In some accounts P'eng-lai is just one seamount, but in
others it is three, each with its own name. As tricorn peaks
they are analogous to and represent the coiffure of the
Royal Mother of the West. In at least one early medieval
source their number has increased to five.[6]

Taoist sources are most circumstantial about the perils of
the approaches to P'eng-lai. One, for instance, says that it
lies over against the northeast shore of the Eastern Sea, that
it is five thousand *li* in diameter, and that it is surrounded
by untraversable black waters, where waves, undriven by
any terrestrial wind, rise thousands of feet. Hence one of
the common names of this dangerous ocean: the Stygian

Sea (*Ming hai*).[7] This is not a very ancient name, but it was a popular one in post-Han times, and we shall see it again in one of Ts'ao T'ang's quatrains.

In addition to the colorless name of Eastern Sea, the medieval Chinese had other names for these waters, into which all rivers poured and which stretched endlessly beyond Japan. They were called the Watchet Sea (*ts'ang hai*), a translation using an uncommon English word to render an uncommon Chinese word that connotes the gray-green or iron-blue aspect of the ocean. However, an anomalous Taoist tale, defying this convention, tells of a Watchet Sea Island in the "north sea," named for the color of the water around it. The rocks of this island are notable for brightly colored minerals, which shine without smelting or polishing. From these, elixirs of immortality may be compounded.[8] It is inhabited, not surprisingly, by transcendent beings.[9] We may take it that this is simply a mutation of the celebrated island of P'eng-lai.

The Eastern or Watchet Sea was also sometimes called Indigo Sea (*pi hai*), but the latter is commonly the name of the more remote waters surrounding Fu-sang. Whether named Indigo or Cyan (perhaps a more exact translation), this dark sea, like the dark depths of outer space, was a poorly illuminated march of the worlds of men and gods. It provided an agreeable image to Taoist poets of the T'ang, such as Wu Yün, who contrasted its shadowy expanse with the brief flashes from the rare auroral liqueurs and rainbow mushrooms created by the vitalizing *yang* lights unavailable to common mortals.[10]

The Watchet Sea had yet another name, also an ancient one. It was and is called Po-hai. *Hai* is "sea." The epithet *po* (Middle Chinese **bwĕt*) carries the semantic freight of "puff up; pop out; burst; explode; bud; bubble; bulge,"

etc. It is an epithet of puffing vapors and pneumas, and of
swelling clouds. An aphelial comet, so far from the sun that
it has not yet formed a tail, is a "*po*-star"—that is, a
star in the form of a strange puff of light, newly visible
among the eternal constellations. *Po* may also refer to a
solid object. For instance, a hemp floret—its newly burst
flower-bud—is called "hemp pop" (*ma po*). (It has
English analogues in "popcorn" and in "maypop.") The expanded, binomial version of the word is semantically identical. *P'eng-po* (M.C. *bung-bwĕt) has been variously defined as "the appearance of cloudy auras when full-blown;
the aspect of [something] raised up by the wind," and so
forth. That is, it describes the rolling, billowing quality of
tenuous objects expanded by unseen forces.[11] A close relation of this alliterative binom is another, *bung-bwĕt,
which has the dictionary definition of "clashing of waves."
But this must be more sharply defined as "water swelling,
bursting, and puffing," and the Po-hai must be the Puffing
Sea or the Bulging Sea, a name which reminds us of Chang-
hai (yielding Arabic *Sankhai*), that is, the Swollen Sea, the
medieval Chinese name for the South China Sea and especially the open ocean, the high main, that leads southward
to the Indies.

But this explosive sea is also the site of a puffed-out seamount. The *p'eng* (*bung) of *p'eng-po* is also the *p'eng* of
P'eng-lai. The two parts of the binom are interchangeable,
although segment *p'eng* has tended to stick with the island,
and segment *po* with the sea. There are other such inter-
changes: the astronomical section of the *Book of Sui*[12]
takes note of a *p'eng*-star, "whose aspect is like powder or
fluff," clearly another name for an embryonic comet or *po*-
star.

Indeed P'eng was by itself sufficient as the name of the

holy isle. So when the poet Ch'en T'ao wrote that he might be thwarted by dust flying around the turtle's feet (images that will be elucidated later), he was referring to "the road to P'eng."[13] But usually the fuller form P'eng-lai is used. Superficially, this is a name without a meaning, although the sense of its first element has now been adumbrated. But there is more to be said about it. The seamount is sometimes described as, or assumed to be, an ordinary island rising from the sea, but sometimes it appears to float on the surface of the ocean, and sometimes to hover over it in the manner of Laputa. The name P'eng is appropriate to such an island, partly because it is an insubstantial puff of mist or cloud, but also because it tosses about aimlessly at the mercy of the wind. To be more precise, the word *p'eng*, used by itself, refers specifically to the Asiatic tumbleweed, an unhappy introduction into North America where Hollywood has embellished it with the flavor of the cowboy myth.[14] It also forms part of the expression *p'ing-p'eng*, which refers to the yellow nuphar or spatterdock, a regular metaphor in Chinese poetry for a person or thing blown about at random, especially by the waves. *P'eng*, with the same overtones as its cousin *po*, is also used of a mop of windblown hair,[15] and is cognate with another *p'eng*, "sail." In short, the word combines the sense of "mop; globular tangle" with that of "floating before the wind."

The meaning of the element *lai* in P'eng-lai is not so obvious, but we have a clue in one of the island's other names—Yün Lai "cloud comes," probably intending "it comes [drifting like a] cloud."[16] Similarly, P'eng-lai may mean "coming [like a windblown] tumbleweed or pond nuphar." Another name is P'eng Hill (*p'eng ch'iu*), that is, Tumbleweed Hill, Drifting Hill, or Windblown Hill.

The name and its aura of meaning leads us even further.

The classic description of the Royal Mother of the West, whose mountain is a mirror-image of P'eng-lai, provides the great goddess with a mop of tousled hair (*p'eng*). It is thus significant that, in a startling poetic image, Li Po compares the crags of P'eng-lai to the hairpins in the coiffure of the giant turtle that carries the island on its head.[17] In fact, the lady was herself the supportive turtle, for we learn in Taoist literature that one of her titles is "Metal Mother of Turtle Mount,"[18] or simply "Turtle Mother."[19] The tossed, tousled island is her chignon and its ornaments.

This cosmic turtle (if the epithet is not too weighty) seems to account for the mobility of the magic island, at least when it is becalmed. At any rate, its base was not always the reptile's gigantic head—sometimes it was the carapace. But, like Li Po, Ts'ao T'ang favored the forward part of the vessel, as demonstrated by the following quatrain:

> The course of one hundred years—to them it is a single
> springtime;
> It is not ever required of sun and moon that they shift their
> wheels.
> In the basilicas of P'eng-lai, on the head of a golden sea-turtle,
> There is no person who did not refine his bones when among
> humankind. (68)[20]

To paraphrase: Among the immortal sylphs, spring is forever; sun and moon do not move; there is no mutation, no decay, no seasonal change. The holy city in the sea is populated entirely by beings who were like you and me, but were wise enough to prepare themselves by synthesizing eternal bodies, through meditation and the absorption of astral essences, while still on earth.

The other point of view is presented by the Taoist poet P'i Jih-hsiu in a fantasy which animates the landscape of the Grand Lake (*t'ai hu*), turning it into a cosmic ocean with all its inhabitants:

> The trees move as if they were the tails of clam-monsters;
> The mountains float, seeming to be the spine of a sea-turtle.[21]

As to what sort of behemoth this turtle was, there are a number of possible answers: it was a cultural import from India, species unknown; it was the work of Chinese mythographers, exaggerating an ordinary marine turtle; it was a somewhat less exaggerated version of the giant leatherback turtle (*Dermochelys coriacea*), which cruises the waters of warm oceans.

The silver chateaus of P'eng-lai, the mystical center of the sea and its floreate borders, housed a clan of angelic beings who may be envisaged in the likeness of the peris of Iran. Little individuality was attributed to them in the earliest accounts. Even when the isle and its inhabitants were assimilated to full-fledged Taoism after Han times, and names and functions were allotted to individuals among them, few had distinct personalities, and they remain hardly distinguishable from the mountain-dwelling "divine persons" described in the ancient book of *Chuang tzu*, a great source of imagery for medieval Taoist writers. They were as delicate as children, nourished only by air and dew, and roved freely above the surface of the earth in cloud-chariots drawn by dragons.[22] They lived in palatial houses built of precious stones and metals—chiefly, it appears, gold and silver—and the supernatural birds and beasts that shared the island with them were as white as they, like the rare albinos of the mainland, whose appearance to human eyes was always taken to be a signal from the divine world.[23]

Early literature has many examples of the strange and

magical things to be found there, some knowledge of which had reached the Middle Kingdom. For example, the rivers that flowed down the slopes of the sea-isle were replete with beautiful luminescent minerals that, without the need of smelting, polishing, or other technology, were already jewels of the highest quality. What is more, these were edible, and the fortunate denizens of the mountain partook freely of them. Presumably the ambrosial minerals were as rarefied and imponderable as the air and dew on which the divine beings of *Chuang tzu* subsisted. P'eng-lai also produced a unique fruit, the eastern counterpart of the celebrated peaches of K'un-lun. This was a life-prolonging melon, known as "Numinous Melon from the Hollow of Space."[24] ("Hollow of Space" refers to the boundless egg in which the Primal Pneumas generated all phenomena.) Comparable marvels occasionally strayed into the world of men. Their very appearance was enough to identify their source. One such marvel is described in a quatrain by the T'ang poet Wei Ying-wu:

> A scarlet tree, without flowers or leaves,
> Neither stone nor yet rose-gem:
> In what place might a man of our world find it?
> It grows on the rocks of P'eng-lai.[25]

This branching, rutilant plant was a specimen of the precious red coral of the distant Mediterranean, an object of amazement to the medieval Chinese to whom its true source was unknown. Occasionally a specimen was brought to the T'ang court by ambassadors from some kingdom of central or southern Asia, who in turn had obtained it from an entrepreneur with agents in unknown lands. To many, it appears, P'eng-lai was its natural home.[26]

The palace of P'eng-lai was governed by a shadowy hierarchy of divinities, whose attributes are recorded only sketchily. Different sources give different titles for their overlord. One such is "Realized King of the Nine Heavens" (*chiu t'ien chen wang*), who governed with the aid of nine elderly viziers.[27] As a "realized person," that is, a being privileged to attend the court of Highest Clarity, he had authority over the merely "transcendent" persons who populate the island. There was also an executive officer, himself a mere transcendent, named Lo Kuang-hsiu.[28] The names of some of the sovereign's ministers are known: Chiang Shu-mao, Chia Pao-an, and Sung Ch'en-yang.[29] None of these personages plays any role in Ts'ao T'ang's poetry, which is always concerned with the flower children—sometimes happy, sometimes melancholy—who divert themselves in the gardens and pavilions on the palace grounds.

P'eng-lai was a paradise rarely seen by the men of old. In medieval times it had become more visible to some. For instance, Ch'ien Liu, ruler of the state of Wu-Yüeh in the tenth century, built a P'eng-lai Gallery at Shao-hsing, presumably with confidence that he would glimpse the island's shining towers out in the sea.[30] The name P'eng-lai was also bestowed on the tropical island of Hainan, just off the coast of southernmost China, a region virtually unknown in antiquity. The equivalence was a profitable one: not long after the fall of T'ang an aloeswood incense made on the island was marketed on the mainland as P'eng-lai Aromatic. In our own century there is a market town there called P'eng-lai, whose name may have some relation to the plan to develop coastal parts of Hainan as a workers' paradise.[31] As of this writing, it seems to be doing fairly well as a tourist resort.

I could be bounded in a nutshell, and count
myself a king of infinite space.

SHAKESPEARE
Hamlet, act 2, sc. 2

The Hollow Worlds

LIKE ALL MOUNTAINS of worth, seamount
P'eng-lai had a secret or "true" shape that was not apparent
from the clusters of silvery houses and golden halls that
encrusted its slopes. This mystical form is expressed in one
of the common names of the island, Tumbleweed Pot
(*P'eng hu*), which evokes an image of a miniaturized world
sufficiently compressible to fit without distortion into a
drinking gourd. Although more portable, this microcosmic
calabash—actually carried about by wandering holy men
as a place of refuge, seclusion, or recreation—is the other-
identity of the grotto-heavens (*tung t'ien*) that lie beneath

the roots of the sacred mountains. The ideal calabash has the form of a double cone, rather like a narrow-waisted drum,[32] symbolizing the opposite realms of *yin* and *yang*, heaven and earth interacting; it was another version of the cosmic egg, the crystal-lined geode, the human skull; all forms of it are equally real. (In schemes that envisage the eastern isle as multiple, one of them regularly bears the name of Square Pot [*Fang hu*], that is, a celestial bubble embedded in the rectangular earth.)[33]

In poetry, Tumbleweed Pot often stands in opposition to the heights of K'un-lun, called either Fells of K'un (*K'un lang*), Winds on the Fells (*Lang feng*), or Park of the Fells (*Lang yüan*). That is, they represent the two extremities of the world, each with its special avenue to the upper realms. The interrelationship is demonstrated in one of Wu Yün's ecstatic visions, where he finds himself at an immense height in the Void, from which the magic mountains of east and west appear as near neighbors:

> Now that I glimpse my nearness to Tumbleweed Pot,
> Who would say that I am far from the Fells of K'un?[34]

Wu Yün's friend Li Po is more earthbound. To him the passage beyond the divine calabash, or as he puts it, "To surmount the sea-towers of Tumbleweed Pot,"[35] is a tremendous leap. A century later Ts'ao T'ang performed his special wizardry on the convex edens of K'un-lun and P'eng, on such concave edens as the star-studded world beneath Mount T'ien-t'ai, and also on the asylum within a magic calabash:

> Mounted on a dragon, he crosses the head of the jade gorge
>   once more;
> Red leaves have reverted to spring, and the cyan water flows.

But he realizes now that a Heaven and an Earth can be seen
    within a pot:
Heaven and Earth within a pot—but not once an autumn. (3)

This may be paraphrased as follows: "A perfected being
guides his serpentine steed over a shining valley; he saw it
last when it was clothed with dying autumn leaves, but
now it sparkles with the runoff from vernal freshets. In the
interval he has been admitted to the mysteries, in particular
to the truth that there are other worlds than this one—
worlds of eternal springtime, and of eternal life." Here
the poet provides neither an exalted perspective reaching
far beyond the antechambers of paradise, nor simply a
charming passage over enchanted seas. He admonishes his
readers to attend to the difference between inevitable
debility and death in one world, and endless springtime in
another.

Such is P'eng-lai: phenomenal aspect and noumenal
aspect; mutable vision and eternal substratum. The question of its genesis and composition remains. An obvious
answer is at hand. Like its crystalline inhabitants, it congealed out of the Primal Pneuma (*yüan ch'i*), the unorgan-
ized anima which gave birth to the eternal deities of Jade
Clarity even before the separation of *yin* and *yang* in the
era of Grand Culmination (*T'ai chi*). Likely as this genesis
is, a somewhat less refined one—one which is more suited
to its appearance than to its substance—was commonly
provided by early literature. It is an emanation or mutation
of water.

In A.D. 382 the ancient metropolis of Ch'ang-an, then
ruled by a dynasty of former border-raiders, was terrified
by the report of a vast expanse of water in its purlieus,
where no water should be.[36] This alarming spectacle was

described, probably not for the first time, as a "water image", where "image" inadequately translates a word that means "light-formed shape" (such as a silhouette, shadow, or reflection).[37] There were other names for this phenomenon. For instance, in a report of A.D. 448 it is called a "ground mirror" (*ti ching*).[38]

It is not surprising that Ts'ao T'ang exploited this illusion in an appropriately fantastic setting. In the following quatrain he tells of a man, perhaps a Taoist adept, who enters a limestone grotto, doubtless in search of a jade woman to initiate him into the techniques of mystic love:

> The stars sink below the trees—the moon aims for the heights;
> In the gorge ahead, watery images wet a dragon's pelt;
> Clouds cool in the grotto-heaven—jade flowers open;
> The lordling wraps himself completely in his double brocaded caftan. (72)

The adit that leads to an underground world shows a pattern of wavering instability. Phantom liquids—perhaps the effect of moonlight—play over the glittering scales of a serpentine spirit. Pale, inorganic flowers enhance the cool imagery of this fantastic scene. The moon approaches the zenith—that is, it is nearly midnight, when the realm of spirits becomes accessible. Everything is quiet, chilly, misty, expectant. The aristocratic apprentice, probably already admitted to the lesser mysteries of Highest Clarity, shivers as he peers into the dark recesses ahead.

Water is always associated with grottoes; it is the lifeblood of these veins and arteries of the earth. We find the bewildering play of images on that deceptive fluid treated in a rather different way in another of Ts'ao T'ang's underground poems. Here, instead of "water images," he writes "river images," using a word reserved for upland streams and rushing waters:

> River images sink in the sand—tree images become clear;
> In men's homes all tread out the course of the pentatones.
> How appealing the roads to the thirty-six heavens!
> Where stars and moon fill all of space, and the rose-gem plants
>   are green. (91)

The scene exemplifies the conjunction of nature with ritual—an essential of Taoist practice. At midnight, when the celebrants trace out the patterns of "Pacing the Void," the shimmering phantoms on the surface of the water disappear and are replaced by the simple reflections of riverside trees. The liturgical music is set in the ancient pentatonic mode. The thirty-six grottoes are the thirty-six "lesser" grotto-heavens beneath the mountains of China, each equipped with its own sky and luminaries.[39]

Perhaps a plausible interpretation of these verses is that Ts'ao T'ang has created an image of the world of men as an unstable illusion and mirage. Men may dance to the old sacred measures, hoping to make themselves eligible to follow the low road to a new heaven and a new earth—and perhaps, but not for certain, up the high road into a cloudless, eternal sky.

From haunted water-vaults emerged the true form of P'eng-lai, a hollow gourd afloat on the world-ocean. To reach this distant island we must take a devious route. We proceed from the dripping limestone caverns of China, by way of the wardrobes of sylphine sea-princesses and their garments made of magical threads, to our destination on the eastern ocean. This detour introduces us to both pelagic weavers and pelagic architects.

Transparent Forms, too fine for Mortal Sight,
Their fluid Bodies half dissolv'd in Light.
Loose to the Wind their airy Garments flew,
Thin glitt'ring Textures of the filmy Dew;
Dipt in the richest Tincture of the Skies,
Where Light disports in ever-mingling Dies.

ALEXANDER POPE
The Rape of the Lock, II, 55–72

Jade Consorts and Pelagic Costumes

AN INITIATE into the secrets of the upper world, ambitious to join its deathless inhabitants, was bound to become familiar with their attributes in order to recognize the status and power of any unearthly figure that might appear to him in a vision. Moreover, just as at a court ball on earth, the perfected beings above found social intercourse much facilitated by a familiarity with the special significance of sashes, epaulets, medals, and the like, in a bewildering variety of materials, shapes, and colors. This essential iconography, documented in bewildering detail in the Taoist scriptures, became the portion of the medieval poets, who plundered the canon for fine phrases to characterize the divine masqueraders with whom they populated their devotional or romanticized poems about the gardens in the sky. They enriched their verses with allusions to the cloud patterns of gowns and slippers, to star-studded crowns, to feathered dresses, fiery amulets, and purple medallions—and much else.

The language of the heraldry of space is virtually inexhaustible. It employs, in part, the language of alchemy, which in medieval Taoism was no simple description of the transmutation of metals; it included the manufacture of models of natural process, cosmic evolution, and somatic circulations, but had many other uses, some of them purely contemplative and beyond the scope of this study.[40] Here we are concerned with the names of the supernatural equivalents of ordinary chemical reagents and their application to the everyday trappings of celestial life. Just as the magical herbs of earth have supernatural and superior analogues, so terrestrial products of mines and metallurgical works were base copies of perfect minerals above the sky. These perfect substances were usually synthesized in celestial workshops: they appear in Ts'ao T'ang's poetry as the acrylics, vinyls, and polyurethanes of the supernal world. From them were fashioned the vestments particularly suited to the class of radiant beings known as "Jade Consorts" (*yü fei*). Indeed, these jewel-like ladies were inseparable from their shimmering costumes.

Jade Consorts are not restricted to Ts'ao T'ang's verses. For instance, in a poem about the great snowfall of A.D. 311, when there were supposed to have been "snow flowers" a foot in circumference, Han Yü has set down the following vision of the event:

> A white nimbus opens up the way ahead—
> Followed by a myriad of jade consorts.[41]

In other words, the soft crystalline flakes resemble a host of sky maidens clad in jade-white costumes. Indeed in this avatar the gemmy creatures are close kin to the white moon-fairies (*su o*) who flit about that satellite, mounted on white birds and dressed in white riding habits.[42]

Personages bearing the title Jade Consort are often, as we should expect, persons of quality. A distinguished member of the coterie is Jade Consort of the Western Numen (*hsi ling yü fei*).[43] Possibly she is the same as Chen Yu-hsiao, the Numinous Consort of Western Florescence (*hsi hua ling fei*).[44] (The Hall of Western Florescence was situated in the realm of Highest Clarity, where it was a residence of Hsi Wang Mu. But its lower counterpart was Mount K'un-lun, and its more earthbound equivalent was Mount Hua, the Marchmount of the West, in China itself.)[45]

A Jade Consort might even be encountered on earth. In a prose account of the search of Li Lung-chi (posthumously T'ang Hsüan Tsung) for the soul of his lost consort—a kind of companionable preface to Po Chü-i's celebrated "Song of Lasting Resentment" (*Ch'ang hen ko*)—that poet's friend Ch'en Hung shows the heavenly house of the divine Lady Yang identified by a placard which styles it "Close of the Most Great Realized One, the Jade Consort" (*Yü fei t'ai chen yüan*).[46] Here the elevated version of Yang Kuei-fei has become another identity of the Royal Mother and simultaneously a member of the class of Jade Women of the most exalted sort.

But most jade consorts are presented to the reader anonymously. Such is the case in one of Ts'ao T'ang's quatrains:

> Within the grotto the moon brightens—rose-gem trees are
>   wind-blown;
> Painted curtains in a blue house—cast-light scarrow.[47]
> Incense fades, wine cools—Jade Consort fallen asleep,
> Unaware that the Seven Realized ones have departed into the
>   sea. (87).

The scene is a divine residence in a grotto-heaven, lit by a moon unknown to us, and animated by divine presences. The party tires, and the great sky lantern dims. The hostess has fallen asleep on the mat and her princely guests steal quietly away. The Seven Realized Ones are identified differently in different lists. For instance, Lu Kuei-meng treats them as the seven founders of Mao Shan Taoism: the three Mao brothers, Yang Hsi, the two Hsü, and Kuo Szu-ch'ao.[48] But elsewhere they are the "Seven Magistrates of the Seven Primes," that is, the rulers of the seven stars of the Dipper.[49]

In marked distinction to these rather queenly images, the immaculate ladies appear somewhat reduced in stature in the following account of the celestial scriptorium, where the Royal Mother of the West is attended by one or more jade consorts:

> The Most Great Realized One plied the brush;
> Jade Consort[s] brushed off her ground-mat.
> Yellow gold made the letters;
> White jade made the plates.[50]

Here our "consorts" are only serving wenches—but of course much more refined than any such on earth. In the same way the title "Consort" was often given to quite lowly persons. The following passage from a sacred scripture shows them in a different role:

> Numinous Consorts (*ling fei*) scatter flowers;
> Golden Lads (*chin t'ung*) elevate censers.[51]

In this case the "consorts" are only little flower girls performing their lowly task as attendants at a grand procession. Similarly in the poems of Ts'ao T'ang the title "consort," more often than not, seems merely to designate a lady-in-waiting, rather than a royal wife as in the secular world—or sometimes a receptionist, or even a scullery maid. In short, most jade consorts are indistinguishable from those ubiquitous beings of Taoist literature, the jade women. Or to put it another way, they are all star women. They are pure, white, and shining, crystallized like snowflakes out of the primordial mist.[52]

Among more formal descriptions of the genesis of jade women we may note two statements of methods whereby adepts may materialize them in deep meditation: "Jade women take shape spontaneously from responsive resonances of the miraculous pneuma,"[53] and "The *yang*-pneuma will transmute to make a dragon carriage; the *yin*-pneuma will alter to make a jade woman."[54] When visiting the earth they have a marked affinity with the summits of sacred mountains. Indeed, some of their number have formed very close relationships with particular mountains. For instance, the Jade Woman of the Luminous Star offers an elixir of immortality to deserving adepts on Mount Hua, the holy mountain of the west.[55] A host of these shining women constitute the court and the palace staff of the Royal Mother of the West. The costumes of two of her personal attendants have been described for us: "When they ascend to the basilica they don crowns tied with Dawn Ribbons of Grand Verity, and are shod with slippers patterned with Phoenixes of the Mystic Rose-Gem."[56] It goes without saying that the delicate creatures also throng the ethereal palaces of the sky.

They are not merely decorative: these star-born princesses had a variety of specialized roles and functions. One task to which many or most of them were assigned was the care of the archives of the stellar palaces, where the perfect originals of the sacred scriptures were stored. It follows that they are also, on occasion, lending librarians, who unshelve and deliver suitable books for the edification of deserving adepts. Here is one of them; she may be taken to typify all of her immortal sisters:

> There is a jade woman within the Purple Chamber of the Six Pairings of the All Highest; she is attendant and guardian of "The Secret Writs of the Grand Cinnabar."[57]

Other roles played by these angels of light derive from this primary function. They are the couriers who transmit the wonderful tablets engraved with true spells, rites, and other procedures for the attainment of a perfect body and endless life among the stars. Accordingly, they were as much teachers as messengers. The bond formed between them and their mortal disciples was as tight as that between bride and bridegroom. They held the master keys which unlock both the bookcases of the gods and the chambers of an adept's heart: love laughs at locksmiths.

The scriptural archetype of the celestial mistress is the

Jade Woman of Greatest Mystery (*T'ai hsüan yü nü*), who is actualized by the adept within the disc of the sun or the moon, immediately in front of his face. She is seen clad in a purple cap, and a skirt and stole of vermilion damask. She exhales a scarlet draught into the mouth of the fortunate adept, in a kind of cosmic kiss. If for a period of five years one follows the techniques which she recommends, she will, the scripture tells us, "come down to you, and lie down to take her ease with you."[58]

As demotic images these damsels resemble sacred brides well enough, but, *sub specie aeternitatis*, they must be regarded as impersonal vessels whose jade-white faces and iridescent costumes are no more than transient phenomena—masks adapted to the limitations of mortal vision. They themselves are lightning conductors that transmit energetic pneumas into the vital organs of the aspiring adept. The count of their population is not known—it may be infinite. The names or titles of a few of them have been preserved. One of the most eminent of these is the Jade Woman of Occult Miracles (*Hsüan miao yü nü*), the mother of Lord Lao. We have both the name and the title of a member of the court of Blue Lad: she is Yen Ching-chu ("Phosphor Orb"), a Jade Woman of the Palace of Eastern Florescence, where she is associated with Blue Lad's younger sister, who enjoys higher rank as "Jade Consort of Eastern Florescence," and is named Ch'un Wen-ch'i.[59] Others are the Jade Woman of the Numinous Forest, the Jade Woman of the Grand Immaculate, the Life-Increasing Jade Woman of the Blue Sky, the Jade Woman of the Divine Cinnabar, and the Jade Woman of the Northern Palace.[60] Some titles refer to whole classes of jade women. For instance, there are a hundred Jade Women of the Three

Heavens.[61] Ten officers of a celestial court are collectively
called Blue-Waisted Jade Women.[62] They are doubtless akin
to the Blue Woman or Blue Women who create frost and
snow.[63] This power is at least in part symbolic; just as they
themselves were congealed out of the primordial nebula, so
they are invested with the power to crystallize the pneumas
that rove the cosmos.

Jade women appear often in the quatrains of Ts'ao
T'ang, but he seldom shows them in their most demanding,
responsible, or exciting roles. They are almost entirely restricted to the status of maidservants in the employ of grand
personages in whose private affairs they have a consuming
interest. They are hardly to be distinguished from his "jade
consorts." They easily fall in love with visiting spirit-lords.
In the following poem we see a Blue-Waisted Woman reduced to a purely menial condition:

> Up in the sky a cock calls—the sun reddens on the sea:
> A blue-waisted serving woman sweeps the Vermilion Palace.
> She washes the flowers, steams leaves, warms clarified wine on
>   a brazier;
> She waits with the Lady to welcome the Five Oldsters. (28)

(The Vermilion Palace is one of several at the Metropolis of
Greatest Mystery [*T'ai hsüan tu*] on the Mountain of the
Jade Capital [*Yü ching shan*], where high celestial digni-
taries convene on the twenty-fourth day of each month to
peruse reports submitted by the spirit-king of the north.
These enumerate the merits of ghosts of former humans
imprisoned in cheerless dungeons.)[64] The story of this
poem tells how, as the sun rises over the Eastern Sea, far
below, a jade maiden begins her daily chores in the palace
of the Cosmocrator. She freshens the flowers, and prepares

tea and wine, anticipating the arrival of the personifications of the Five Planets (who attended the birth of Confucius) now coming to visit her august mistress.

In another quatrain, the delicate creature—this time not of the blue-waisted variety—has given her lowly heart, like an eighteenth-century serving wench, to a noble guest, believing him incapable of wrong, no matter how faithless he may appear:

> A crane in the clouds, in stygian darkness—its departure
>   indistinct;
> Fallen flowers drift with the water—rancor remains—in vain.
> [But] he is unaware of the termless trust of a Jade Woman,
> Who spoke with him on leaving the gate open—or shutting
>   the gate. (48)

This high-flying, nearly invisible bird is certainly Wang Tzu-ch'iao, the were-crane, whom we shall encounter later as a great lover. He is aiming for his home in the northeast, just as the rivers of China flow eastward, away from life and love, to eternal extinction in the sea, carrying broken blossoms with them—remnants of a lady's love token. The demigod is oblivious of a maidservant who believes him incapable of deserting her mistress—but he paid her no attention when she asked him whether or not she should leave the door ajar for his return.

A jade woman need not be actually designated as such. Her quality can be determined from her circumstances, as in the following vignette:

> The Jade Resplendent One has conferred a purple dress and
>   petticoat on his handmaiden:
> He instructed me to go over to the Font of Peaches—to wed
>   Esquire Juan.

I have macerated rose-gem flowers in a brew, which I shall
  urge my lord to sip,
Fearing lest my lord's furry sideburns, unawares, become
  frosted. (23)

Some explication is necessary. The Jade Resplendent One
(*Yü huang*)[65] rules the cosmos from its summit over the
Pole Star. Purple is the polar color and appropriate for a
gift from that mighty lord. "Dress and petticoat" is an old
cliché for the basic Chinese costume, without frills; it consisted of an undergarment extending from armpits to an-
kles, covered by an outer tunic or frock, visible to the world.
The Font of Peaches (*T'ao yüan*) originally referred to an
isolated enclave of innocent survivors from an earlier age,
uncontaminated by progress and corruption. They are the
product of the imagination of the poet T'ao Ch'ien. In
T'ang Taoist poetry—here, for instance—the name has
been assimilated to another myth, that of the admirable
youth Esquire Juan, placed in the remote canyons of
Mount T'ien T'ai. "Rose-gem flowers" are still unidentified, but are said to have been rare fragrant yellow
blooms; in Ts'ao T'ang's verses they are a food of long
life.[66] We may paraphrase this quatrain as follows:

The Universal King has bestowed a truly royal outfit upon a
  palace girl,
As a wedding gift—since he is sending her down to earth as
  the bride of the young demigod Juan Chao.
She takes with her a rare elixir
To make sure that old age never creeps up on him.

The potion will assure the elevation of the younger man to
the status of a demigod, but even then the draught will
need renewal to prevent creeping old age. This is a charac-

teristic theme of Ts'ao T'ang's Taoist poems: even the
Gods grow old, like the Aesir of Asgard. But their time is
not our time, though in the end they must succumb to the
eternal cycle of cosmic seasons.[67]

Another quatrain provides a closer look at a costume
suitable for a celestial maiden:

> Her petticoat sewn of blue damask, with bangles of green
> jade;
> Her whole person newly zoned with "Five Cloud Aromatic";
> Relaxed, she ascends a simurgh-borne equipage, and taking
> the Cyan Sea [route],
> Smiling, she goes off to Lord Su to seek a taste of his tanger-
> ines. (30)

Here the blue damask, the green jade, and the Cyan Sea are
all associated by color with the magical realms of the east,
that is, with P'eng-lai and Fang-chu. The "Five Cloud
Aromatic," presumably flashing with the magical hues of
each part of the cosmos, has no earthly counterpart; but
the unidentified lady conforms to earthly fashion: in T'ang
times women of the upper classes were festooned with
scent bags and sachets filled with exotic aromatics, Borneo
camphor being one of the most popular. Lord Su is the
wonder-worker Su Lin. An old tale tells that he was able to
cure victims of an epidemic disease with a single leaf from
his tangerine tree and a gill of water from his well.[68] In Mao
Shan Taoism he became a great divinity of the Grand Culmen (*T'ai chi*) realm, elevated from the rank of a "Jade
Esquire" charged with the surveillance of the Five Marchmounts (*wu yüeh*), that is, the limits of the inhabitable
world.[69] His tangerines are a variety of sourpeel tangerine,
whose most famous subspecies is the kumquat (*chin
chüeh*), the golden sourpeel for which Mount Lo-fou in
Kwangtung is famous.[70]

This poem, then, tells of a grand dame of the eastern ocean, richly garbed and scented, possibly a relative or associate of Blue Lad. She flies across the Watchet Sea for a refreshing picnic with a distinguished spirit-lord on the mainland.

A splendid royal robe of imperishable nylon seems to appear in another of Ts'ao T'ang's quatrains:

> The wind grows cool on the Eight Seas—aqueous images rise high:
> An exalted steward requires the tailoring of a Red Frost Caftan.
> Kraken silk and threads of jade are hard to cut to pattern;
> They need to borrow golden knives and shears from the Jade Consort. (96)

Here the notion of "aqueous images" is not restricted to transient patterns on the surface of land or water, as in a quatrain translated earlier. Out on the sea it had grander manifestations: the expression refers to phantom buildings glittering offshore, as will appear in the next section of this study. The title "Exalted Steward" is not necessarily specific, but may allude to the oldest of the Mao brothers, eponymous founders of the Mao Shan sect—that is, to Mao Ying.[71] The Eight Seas are the orderly array of pelagic waters, corresponding to the cardinal and intermediate points of the compass. The marvelous caftan referred to here deserves a digression. It is the particular and private robe of the Lady of Highest Prime (*Shang yüan fu-jen*), one of the most important goddesses of the Highest Clarity communion of Taoism.[72] In her hieratic aspect, dressed in her unique cloak and invested with other attributes of power and glory, she might easily pass as the most exalted of the seraphim:

She is costumed in a Red Frost Caftan, overlapped with a cape of blue-plumed damask. A tricorn chignon is built on her head, and her loose hair reaches to her waist. She is crowned with the crown "Night Moon in the Primal Daybreak." She is belted with the girdle of "Fire Jade of the Six Mountains," and at her waist is the Grand Ribbon with Phoenix Pattern and Sapphire Flowers. She holds the Sword of Fluid Yellow and Pulsating Phosphors.[73]

This handsome apparition, which had amazed kings and prophets in earlier times, became the common property of medieval poets. The divine Li Po knew her well. In an artfully contrived poem about her he begins with a recapitulation of exactly the splendid blazonry presented in the text above, and calls her, in her enchanting beauty, the peer of the Royal Mother herself. But he deprives her of some of her sources of authority, such as the magic sword, and gives her instead a young girl as a companion: the elusive pair whirls off into the aether with enigmatic smiles, to the elfin sounds of panpipes.[74]

As for the fabric of the fantastic caftan, it was the product of a supernal alchemy. Even the experiments of terrestrial adepts employed and produced all sorts of delicate compounds that dazzled the eyes of the initiate with visions of infinity and convinced him of the mutability of all things. To all of these attractive products of the worldly laboratory there were celestial equivalents which had existed from the beginning of time. One of these was "red frost" which, from its color, was a kind of crystallized *yang* plasma, analogous to the many "frosts" and "snows" produced in the athanors of earth. Usually they were ephemeral compounds of mercury, lead, copper, and arsenic, twinkling on many-colored tinsel crusts—blazons of the power within the crucible itself. The Lady was wrapped in a robe inexplicably woven of incredible threads of softened cinnabar or malleable realgar. As to the "golden" cutting tools required to work the fabric, the epithet "golden" is probably a shortening of "Golden Rigidity" (*Chin kang*), a name for the diamond borrowed into Chinese from Indic sources. In Chinese tradition, diamonds were noted more for their hardness than for their beauty.[75] Above all, they were honored as the sole natural substance that could slice through jade, and jade-cutting tools had a special affinity with the world mountain, K'un-lun.

The elegant quatrain of a few pages back may accordingly be paraphrased along the following lines:

> Supernatural cold blows over the circumambient ocean, among the phantoms created by the lords of the water;
> A celestial seneschal, anticipating a grand ball and reception at a sacred seamount, sends someone to obtain the incomparable scarlet cloth needed to make a warm robe for a goddess.
> This excellent material is supple and strong, as befits the costume of an immortal being,
> Indeed, so tough that it can be cut only by diamonds from the workshops of heaven.

Such costumes as these, presumably fashioned from "frosts," "snows," and other crystalline forms of water cooked in divine retorts and flasks, were, as Ts'ao T'ang's poem shows, akin to if not identical with the miraculous "kraken silk" woven by mermaids—purveyors to the royalty of P'eng-lai. We shall soon see their workshops under the Eastern Sea.

The creatures dipped their fingers in the water, and from the drops they pulled thread which they deftly wove into a fine soft fabric.... He examined it, marveling at the suppleness of the cloth and its lucent shimmer.

JACK VANCE
The Eyes of the Overworld

... Towns and towers and parapets, rising above the horizon, transforming, crumbling, fairy-like scenes, producing a deep sense of happiness and an endless longing—*fata morgana*! No wonder that these observations, already so beautiful in themselves, have been adorned by the fancies of poetry and folklore.

M. MINNAERT
The Nature of Light and Colour in the Open Air

Clam Castles and the Fata Morgana

THE "AQUEOUS IMAGES" that furnish the backdrop to the Masque of the Red Frost Caftan are neither sensory sheets of water on dry land, nor kaleidoscopic reflections trembling on lakes and rivers. They are oceanic spires and pavilions, offshore visions of fairy castles in the sky—in short, the fata morgana.[76] These haunting panoramas were known by other names in medieval Chinese literature. The most common was a phrase which I shall translate "clam-monsters' towers," representing Chinese *ch'en lou*. "Aqueous images" is the genus; "clam-monsters' towers" is the species. But the word rendered "towers" does not necessarily connote slimness and verticality, such as characterize spires and minarets, but stands for multistoreyed buildings of any shape.

The original sense of the word *ch'en* was "a large bivalve mollusc."[77] In antiquity the flesh was pickled,[78] and there are many pre-Han sources that tell of the use of its shell as a utensil. It was also burnt to make lime for plaster and the like. The molluscan credentials of the creature are impeccable. Other senses of *ch'en* emerged in later times, although the basic meaning persisted alongside them.[79] In imaginative literature particularly, but also in some soberer sources, the mollusc acquired more extravagant attributes. It was transformed into a monster lurking in dark lairs—mysterious submarine grottoes—where it assimilated some of the traits of a sea-dragon, brooding over hidden treasure, frothing at its ambiguous mouth, and belching bubbles into the world of man, in a way somewhat reminiscent of the occidental dragon, crouched over its kingly hoard, spouting puffs of smoke and fire. So well fixed was this image by medieval times that it could be used as an image transferred to a sadistic tyrant, slobbering over the dismal fate of his victims:

> [He] worked his jowls and dripped saliva, gaping and sucking, so that people took him to be a veritable sea-basilisk or dragon-clam.[80]

The dragon-clam in this translation corresponds to *ch'en*, otherwise "clam-monster." The Chinese word is cognate to another *ch'en*, which represents the so-called "dragon" of the zodiacal cycle—that is, the twelve-year Jupiter cycle of Chinese astrology. In short, our familiar "dragon" of street processions was originally a cold, glabrous sub-aqueous monster. (The "sea-basilisk" of the quotation above is the Chinese *chiao*, whom I shall subsequently call "kraken"; he is often associated with the dragon-clam.)

As a species of dragon (*lung*), or with draconic attributes grafted to his clammy nature, the monstrous *ch'en*-clam was already noticed in the ancient philosophical treatise *Huai nan tzu*.[81] Even a twelfth-century text takes note of this equivocal zoology, but that medieval authority favors classical taxonomy and regards the *ch'en* as indeed giant clams, not "dragons" (*lung*). This was probably already a minority view. Late medieval opinion favored a *ch'en* in draconic or serpentine form, with ears, horns, and red dorsal bristles. Although the latter view is markedly different from that of ancient times,[82] some draconic attributes, such as the association with water and aqueous mansions, were actually very old.

In medieval times these taxonomic enigmas were regarded as a subspecies of "kraken" (*chiao*). A sixteenth-century authority on such matters states firmly that "*ch'en* belong in the category of 'krakens.'"[83] I have not seen this relationship stated quite so categorically in T'ang literature, but the two creatures are regularly paired off together in both T'ang and pre-T'ang poetry. Here is such a pairing from the sixth century:

> Pneumas of clam-monsters generate high buildings afar;
> Kraken-people do underwater weaving close in.[84]

It appears that the somewhat more domesticated "kraken-people" (whose name also suggests "shark people")[85] held the inshore waters of the continental shelf, while the clam-monsters were masters of the main. The matching remained constant and common in T'ang times. For instance,

> The water clears, to expose the kraken-men's buildings;
> The hazes melt, to clot into the clam-monsters' towers.[86]

Here the comparison emphasizes the difference between the two kinds of edifice—one sort patiently built underwater, the other molded on the surface from the exhalations of deep-sea creatures.

Here, in a poem addressed to a friend departing for Korea by ship, the kraken-houses and the clam-towers become truly uncanny:

> Nocturnal eyes in the houses of kraken-people: *yin*-fires are cool;
> Surprise moorings at the towers of clam-monsters: auroras of daybreak recede.[87]

(*Yin*-fire is organic phosphorescence: the white eyes of the pelagic krakens gleam coldly from their windows.)

In Ts'ao T'ang's glamorous poem about the Red Frost Caftan, the fabric is a divine version of the "silk" or "pongee" woven by the kraken-people. These merfolk wove its prototype under the sea of the Gulf of Tonkin. They were protectors of the Vietnamese, but by T'ang times had been assimilated to northern dragon lore, and the Chinese sometimes treated them as bloodthirsty witch-women rather than the sweet daughters of tropical sea-kings. The manufacture of the shimmering cloth was attributed to these submarine artificers. In fact, the material was imported into China from the coast of the South China Sea, and was well known in both east and west Asia in early times. It was manufactured by very ordinary mortals from

pinikon, the cinnamon-gold threads that anchor the mussel
Pinna squamosa to rocky coasts.[88] The divine agent of
Ts'ao T'ang's quatrain was sent out into the realm of the
clam-monsters to shop for this precious fabric in the
evanescent markets[89] of the great pelecypods—the neighbors of the kraken-weavers.

Other water animals, authentic fleshly creatures, had
other associations with the giant clams. One such was the
Chinese alligator, which haunts the waters of the Yangtze
basin—a mutant dragon. For instance,

> The sun on the lake seems to darken—the alligator drums
> resound;
> The clouds on the sea have just risen—clam-monsters' towers
> abound.[90]

This couplet is marked by the unusual matching of a fresh-
water reptile with the saline mollusc. But there are grounds
for withholding criticism. The alligator was a supernatural
rain-bringer: when, driven by mating fervor—if alligators
may be said to be fervid—it bellowed from its bankside
burrow in the late spring, just as the drenching monsoons
were swelling northward from the topical seas, people
naturally assumed that it was a real dragon calling up the
fertilizing rain from his lacustrine crypt. In ancient rain-
making ceremonies this numinous voice had been imitated
by beating drums—drums covered, for verisimilitude and
effective imitative magic, with alligator hides. In our couplet the crypto-dragons are called from their winter sleep
beside Lake Tung-t'ing (as it may be) to make the nimbus
clouds swell, just as the clam-monsters of the Eastern Sea
churn up magical sky-castles on the surface of the deep.

Poetry also often shows these weird creatures in the
company of the great humped "whale waves" (*ching po*)

that sweep the high seas—swells and surges hardly distinguishable from the great fin, humpback, and sperm whales
who hump along off the coasts of Japan and China. In
short, the affinity of monstrous mammals of the ocean,
breaking the water's surface like newborn islands, with the
giant molluscs who generate sea castles among them, was
clearly recognized by the poets of T'ang—Tu Fu among
them.[91] These waters, then, were true "whale roads" (as in
the Old English kenning) as much as they were the haunts
of the more static shark/kraken people and the benthic
clam-monsters.

To the medieval Chinese, these creative prodigies of the
deep were chiefly associated with the sea-lanes leading to
Korea and Japan in the east—although all of them had
lesser associations with the South China Sea:

> The Enceinte of the Five Goats stands beside the high halls of
> the Clam-monsters.[92]

(The Enceinte of the Five Goats was the walled town of
Canton.)

Many poems were written as tributes to travelers about
to cross to those seagirt realms. They were chiefly natives
heading homeward, but occasionally Chinese envoys on
special missions. We find the fantastic constructions of the
clam-monster, for instance, in an octave of farewell written
in the eighth century by Ch'ien Ch'i to a friend departing
for Japan on such a mission. His ship will take him past
mysterious places:

> Cloud pendents will invite to the seamounts of the transcen-
> dents.
> Rainbow banners will pass by the high halls of the clam-
> monsters.[93]

These verses suggest that the seafarer will catch faint glimpses of two phantom paradises hovering over the waves—the nacreous homes of the winged beings who constitute the lowest order of Taoist supermen, and the frothy citadels of the draconic kings of the ocean. In the ninth century, the Mao Shan poet P'i Jih-hsiu addressed a like prophecy to a Japanese monk he was seeing off on his way back home:

> You may take scriptures from the bottom of the sea, and open
> the dragons' stores;
> You may chant dharanis into space, to scatter the clam-
> monsters' towers.[94]

Here the dragon-clams' towers sound positively menacing, like the magic castles of the demoniac King of Elfland. In any case, these spectral towers were magnificent creations, as Li Shang-yin testifies, in flattering praise of the splendid new pavilion of a lord of T'ang, which puts even the clam-monsters' cloud castles to shame:

> The clam-monsters in the sea, astounded afar, blush to shape
> their towers.[95]

Dangerous and difficult of access perhaps, and gossamer—but they were as gorgeous as anything conjured up by Prospero:

> The cloud-capp'd towers, the gorgeous palaces,
> The solemn temples ...
> ... shall dissolve
> And, like this insubstantial pageant faded,
> Leave not a rack behind.[96]

Flimsiness was not incompatible with reality. The poets emphasize, over and over, that the elaborate edifices on the sea were built from *ch'i*—that is, breath, vital spirit, pneuma—and it is clear that this plastic gas was akin to or identical with the Primal Pneuma out of which the cosmos originally took shape. It was the ultimate stuff of creation.

Clam-monsters, then, are manifestations of an aspect of creative power, and their architectural creations are identical with the palaces of the gods beyond the stars—which are themselves daedalian warps and labyrinthine kinks knotted into the universal homogeneous nebula. The breathy nature of their artifacts—veritable pneumatomorphs—was well established by early Han times: "Beside the sea the breath of clam-monsters is heaped into tall buildings and their platforms."[97]

In T'ang poetry, leaving aside the starry confections of Ts'ao T'ang—the image of these mazy constructs dominates oceanic poetry. In a lively seascape, the seventh-century writer Hsü Ching-tsung, who was much bemused by meteorological and celestial events, matched the clam castles with the invigorating light of the dawn:

> Astounding surges swallow the watchtowers of the clam-
>   monsters;
> Leaping whitecaps cover the light of daybreak.[98]

In an account of various oceanic apparitions of numinous origin, Wang Wei notes that the breathings of black clam-monsters form clouds,[99] but it is not certain that *all* of these creatures are black.

These "leviathans" and their buoyant buildings had some role in the magical arts, as we learn from a late T'ang book of wonders. It tells of an aromatic wax candle belonging to a princess of the household of I Tsung (reigned 860–873). Somehow pigments were introduced into its body in

such a way that its smoke assumed colorful forms of towers, galleries, platforms, and basilicas. There were persons
who alleged that this art, or enchantment, was based on the
blending of clam-monster's fat into the wax of the taper.[100]

Wind-tossed P'eng-lai itself was an impalpable confec-
tion of mists and vapors, analogous to the fuming illusions
formed by the enchanted candle. Since early Han times it
was believed that its white inhabitants performed their
mysterious errands and played their esoteric games in
palaces of gold and silver. These were not substances produced in terrestrial mines, but transient appearances
assumed by vital airs:

> Yellow gold and silver make its palaces and watchtowers, but
> seen from far off, before ever reaching there, they are like
> clouds.[101]

This imagery, like so much else of the language of dreams,
was assimilated to the diction of Taoism. We may read
in Tu Kuang-t'ing's collection of biographies, which is
included in the canon itself, of a divine child who was
brought up in an environment of strange clouds and
pneumas, and lights and phosphors, which were thought
to be manifestations of P'eng-lai or K'un-lun—that is,
formed of subtle vapors.[102] Even secular poetry exploited
the image of the island paradise as a coagulation of fleeting
plasmas, as when Li Shang-yin wrote of "the hazes and
auroras of P'eng Seamount."[103]

But even granted that the holy isle is compounded and
shaped from a pliable ectoplasm, the question remains: is
there a real affinity between the glittering, foamy, transient
sea-palaces inflated by monstrous molluscs and the dazzling white, cloud-covered islands where jadelike youths

dance in eternal innocence? In short, is wave-tossed P'eng-lai the creation of inhuman kings who lurk among the green corals and sea-wracks? There are some very good clues. For instance, the eighth-century pharmacologist Ch'en Ts'ang-ch'i describes a sea creature called *ch'e ao*, which means "carriage *ao*," and our learned authority identifies this as a *ch'en*, that is, a clam-monster. As to the word *ao* itself, in some contexts it refers to the chela of crustaceans, in others to certain bivalve molluscs, but it is particularly noteworthy that it is a clear cognate of *ao*, the name of the giant sea-turtle which carries the magic island of P'eng-lai over the waves. Ts'ang-ch'i goes on to say of this gyral clam-turtle (both creatures are roughly disc-shaped, although the Giant Leatherback—if that reptile indeed underlies the *ao*-turtle—is a shield-like oval) that "it is able to spurt out pneumas to form high buildings and platforms." [104] Here, then, is a clear link between the cloud-wrapped, castled seamount, and its reptilian vehicle, and the splendid halls generated by the great, frothing bivalves. A poem written by Hsü Ning in the ninth century is even more explicit about the connection. It is another farewell stanza addressed to a Japanese envoy returning to his homeland:

> Whale waves rear up over the Archives of the Water;
> Clam-monster pneumas strengthen the Palaces of the Transcendents. [105]

Both submarine archives and sylphine mansions, which keep eternal secrets safe, are the evanescent manufactures of the great, gasping animals in the caverns of the Deep, just as their enchanted robes are the work of another race of sea creatures.

She comes!—the GODDESS!—through the
    whispering air,
Bright as the morn, descends her blushing car;
Each circling wheel a wreath of flowers
      intwines,
And gem'd with flowers the silken harness
    shines;
The golden bits with flowery studs are deck'd
And knots of flowers the crimson reins connect.
And now on earth the silver axis rings,
And the shell sinks upon its slender springs;
Light from her airy seat the Goddess bounds,
And steps celestial press the pansied grounds.

ERASMUS DARWIN
The Botanic Garden, Part I, Canto I, 59–68

Miss Hemp

THERE ARE LINKS between the happy isles
and the unhappy mainland: established routes, and personages who travel them regularly. When in China these
wayfarers appear as almost ordinary human beings—but in
their sea-palaces they have more glorious bodies. The
names of some of these visitors are important, both in
ancient legend and in the medieval vision of P'eng-lai. Of
these the most important is Miss Hemp (Ma Ku). Ts'ao
T'ang wrote a poem about one of her periodic visits to the
mortal world. The occasion was a rendezvous with her old

friend, the divine Wang Yüan, at the house of a certain
Ts'ai Ching who is himself destined for transcendence:

> A pleasant wind blows in the trees—apricot flowers are
>   odorous;
> Under the flowers—a realized person: he says his name is
>   Wang.
> Dragons and serpents in Great Seal graphs attend his brush
>   and billets;
> Starry dippers in small skies cover his gown and skirt.
> He left South Culmen at leisure—the hour of his return will
>   be late:
> He points to East Stygia with a smile, drinking long—exalted.
> He requires that Miss Hemp be called on to join him in a
>   drinking bout;
> They send someone to purchase wine, off in Yü-hang.[106]

A line-for line paraphrase follows:

1 Wind is numinous: a spirit is present; apricot blossoms are
   erotic.
2 The divinity makes his appearance.
3 He is an accomplished writer of spells in the grand style.
4 Like those of any sorcerer, his robes are decorated with the
   images of powerful astrological configurations.
5 He arrives late, having protracted his leisure at the cosmic
   source of rejuvenation in the hot focus of *yang*.
6 He is quaffing elixirs now at the house of Ts'ai Ching. He
   gestures towards the Eastern Sea—where his mystic lady-
   love dwells.
7 He commands that she be sent for; he is ready.
8 But for such a reunion only the best wine will do—the
   wine that the Royal Mother of the West requires, obtain-
   able only in Hangchou.[107]

The unadorned version of Ma Ku's story, which underlies this and many other poems like it, has been often reported. It may be retold briefly here.[108] The fortunate Ts'ai

Ching lived in the Wu region—that is, in the modern province of Chekiang. The demigod Wang Yüan appeared at his house with a splendid retinue, and announced the imminent arrival of the mysterious Miss Hemp. When she appeared radiantly out of the clouds, Miss Hemp wore the aspect of a lovely damsel of eighteen or nineteen. Her hair was partly done up in a chignon, the rest left free to hang down to her waist. She was dressed in an unearthly fabric that shone with a dazzling polychrome light. She was handsomely received, and her delicate palate honored with a meal of fragrant flowers. Now comes the crux of the tale: The lady says to Wang Yüan, "Since I last attended on you, the Eastern Sea has thrice become mulberry fields. Recently I was in P'eng-lai. Then the water was shallower than in previous days: it must be that the period is about half over. Surely it has not become hilly ground once more?" Yüan informs the goddess that the sea has indeed dried up: clearly she has been too engrossed in exalted affairs to notice how advanced the dessication was.

Ts'ao T'ang has focused on the romantic aspects of the impending interview, and says nothing of the dramatic transformation of the Watchet Sea into a sandy desert. But that part of the story receives ample attention from him elsewhere in his writings, as we shall see. For the moment, let us take a closer look at Miss Hemp.

Miss Hemp's particular physical attributes, shown especially in the stunning beauty that is common to these Taoist nymphs, show marked resemblance to those of her female colleagues. Like the Lady of Highest Prime she is described as a lovely girl of eighteen or nineteen, and her coiffure is the same. The two divine women are virtually interchangeable, but Miss Hemp has an attribute all her own—birdlike claws,[109] in which she is akin to a harpy or siren, although she lacks the malevolence of either.

It is not obvious what kind of bird has contributed to Miss Hemp's peerless physique, but there is some evidence that she is a crane-woman. With that uniquely Taoist bird she shares not only the clawed feet but also the repeated voyages across the Eastern Sea—the route of the regular migrations of the sacred red-crowned crane between China and its breeding grounds in Manchuria. Miss Hemp's transits are also seasonal—but they follow the immensely long seasonal cycles of the immortal world. In one of his east-oriented quatrains Ts'ao T'ang lends some confirmation to the hypothesis of her gruine nature:

> Told to forsake the Watchet Sea—could not do it;
> But reliance on simurgh or crane followed instantly!
> The new matron of the Ts'ai household, by no means offended
>   by [their gifts'] paucity:
> Accepts them—and gains three to five pints of true pearls. (90)

The scenario here appears to be as follows: A personage out in the mystic isles has been invited to attend a reception at Ts'ai Ching's household—it can hardly be anyone but Blue Lad, divine ruler of the eastern seas. But he is detained by other business. However, he transmits rare treasures from his aqueous realm by sacred bird-messenger as a gift for the young wife of Ts'ai Ching's brother, who has just borne a son. In the original story the pearls are the gift of Miss Hemp, who magically transmutes grains of cereal into pearls for her host's nephew.[110] In Ts'ao T'ang's poetic version she is only the agent of a distinguished resident of

P'eng-lai—*she* is the crane who transports them across the waves. The ancient crane-road has achieved a glorious fulfillment as the road of the divine bird-woman.

Nonetheless, in surviving literature the venust[111] Miss Hemp exists chiefly as a stock figure to remind us of the periodic slow draining of the Watchet Sea and its refilling. She is almost a personification of cosmic time, measuring off the thousands of years that pass between each flooding. We ourselves are inclined to compare these slow changes to the shifting of waters over continents, corresponding to the melting of the polar ice-caps, which alternates with ice ages during which these incalculable amounts of water are tied up in widespread glaciers, while the shallow seas drain away from the great plains—as they did in Kansas and Texas.[112] Indeed even in medieval China some note was taken of paleontological fact apparently related to the rise and fall of coastal waters. Yen Chen-ch'ing, the eighth-century writer on many Taoist themes, in an account of his visit to an "altar of the transcendents"—specifically the stage for Taoist rituals on Miss Hemp's mountain in what is now Kiangsi Province—retells the old tale of the divine lady and the oscillation of sea level. Then he goes on to describe the rocks in the vicinity of her altar: "in the stone there are still the shells of sea-snails and oysters, possibly transformed in the Mulberry Plantations."[113] It appeared to him that not only had the sea bottom been exposed, but it had also been mysteriously uplifted.

Indeed, a personal cult of Miss Hemp flourished in T'ang times, associating her with rocks, mountains, mysterious grottoes. On the level of popular religion her name was given to a cliff at Mount T'ien T'ai, the holy mountain of Chekiang: the Precipice of Miss Hemp (Ma Ku Yen) was believed to be the very place where she condescended to visit the home of Ts'ai Ching, and in Sung times there was still an old statue of her standing in a grotto there.[114] But in the arcana of Highest Clarity her petrological associations were even more refined: The twenty-eighth of the thirty-six "lesser" grotto-heavens, called "Heaven of the Cinnabar Aurora" (*Tan hsia t'ien*), was believed to lie beneath the mountain in Kiangsi that bears her name, on which the commemorative stele with an inscription composed by Yen Chen-ch'ing was placed. Sovereign in this underworld was the divine Wang Yüan. Moreover, the cavernous tunnel leading to it, the "Grotto of the Cinnabar Aurora," the tenth of the Fortunate Lands (*fu ti*), was recognized as the sanctum where Ts'ai Ching had achieved the Tao, and over which he, in his new body, presided. It was reported that on rainy nights the haunting music of bells and lithophones could be heard there.[115] Nearby, in the offing of Mount T'ien T'ai, was the second of the thirty-six lesser heavens, the Grotto-Heaven of Tumbleweed Mystery (*P'eng hsüan tung t'ien*),[116] perhaps the antechamber to the passage taken by Miss Hemp on some of her many journeys between P'eng-lai and the mainland.

In T'ang poetry, the pelagic cycle of wet and dry is represented as a tidelike ebb and flow, corresponding to very slow changes in the endless lives of the perfected beings of Taoism. These are analogous to the ordinary seasonal changes experienced by mortal men. The cosmic spring brings the onset of the energetic, fertilizing *yang* energy that, at its height, completely eliminates the waters of the ocean—the visible emblem of *yin*, the moist, receptive principle. This slow, dreamlike dessication culminates with the millennial flourishing of the mulberries on the ocean shore and even on its now revealed bed, as well as the flowering of the peach trees that represent eternal life. Then, when the wheel of time completes another half-turn, the cosmic autumn and winter take control of the supernal world, while the inky flood of *yin* once more dominates the pelagic basins. The phrase "mulberry plantations" accordingly takes on a melancholy sense of mortality and transience: the great cyclic catastrophes are temporal flickers that bring little more than a sense of unease to the beings who dwell beyond the stars, but outlast by far the mayfly duration of human life.

A number of Ts'ao T'ang's fantasies touch on these matters. Here is one such:

> Water fills the Mulberry Fields—the white sun sinks;
> Frozen clouds and dry graupel wet the double-layered shade.
> A visitor returning to Liaotung crosses leisurely over them;
> A reason to talk about the Yao years, when the snow was even
>   deeper. (65)

This is a story of the crane-route over the Eastern Sea to Manchuria. The world is in the grip of winter; *yin* emanations, dark and damp, dominate the great ocean. The migrant holy bird—perhaps the celebrated were-crane Ting Ling-wei—flies back to his summer home, signaling the approach of spring and the augmentation of the influence of *yang*, not yet detectable by men. From his high vantage, the venerable creature sees the sun sink into the frozen mountains of the west, and the sea in the east still dominated by the dark vapors of winter. Gloom and chill still prevail everywhere. But for him, this is merely a matter for gossip. When he arrives home he will report his observations to his comrades, and they will chat about the great

snows of prehistory, such as those of the golden age of the
hero Yao, when winters were even more bitter than now—
but there was always a vernal aftermath and the renewal of
life.[117]

In the next two poems, Ts'ao T'ang takes note of a dis-
agreeable aspect of eternal life: the fortunate adept must
endure the sight of his friends, who failed to dedicate their
earthly careers to the cultivation of the potentiality for
permanence, as they wither and blow away in what to him
is but a moment.

> Ch'ang-fang, a natural nobleman, knew how to fly and flutter;
> In the midst of pentachromatic clouds he shuts a gate on him-
>   self.
> He watches the Mulberry Fields off there—due to become a
>   sea;
> He does not know how many persons will have survived
>   when he goes back. (52).

Pi Ch'ang-fang was a master of space and time who had
learned that craft from the master of all masters, the Sire of
the Pot (Hu Kung). This great Taoist art worked in two
complementary ways. The adept could, at will, pass into an
ordinary gourd, which was in fact a vast world populated
by divine beings. Contrariwise, he could reduce a large
territory to the size of a postage stamp, examine it in its
entirety, and then inflate it to its original extent.[118] Ch'ang-
fang was also gifted with the art of flight, which enabled
him to visit secret lodgings hidden within the multicolored
mists and glows of outer space. From such high vantages he
could watch the millennial flooding of the Eastern Sea—no
tedious affair since human time was greatly accelerated for
him—while meditating solemnly on the many generations

of men that had passed into nothingness during his brief
holiday among the nebulae.

The same dismal facet of endless existence is treated differently in the following quatrain:

> Shu-ch'ing gazes all around at springtime under the Nine
>   Heavens;
> Among men he sees not one of the old friends of yesterday.
> Uncanny! He finds the waters below P'eng-lai
> Half turned to sandy soil, half turned to dust. (44)

The protagonist is Wei Shu-ch'ing, who achieved immortality in remote antiquity by the ingestion of mica. Later,
clad in a dress of feathers and a crown of stars, he appeared
to Liu Ch'e (posthumously Wu Ti), the great ruler of Han,
declaring himself to be the tutelary spirit of a mountain.[119]
In this poem he appears in more splendid medieval guise—
a welcome guest at the glittering palace of P'eng-lai. He is
revealed peering through all the worlds, unable to trace the
whereabouts of his erstwhile companions. He is astonished
(perhaps this is forgivable if we imagine him to have
attained transcendence only recently) to find that the seas
around P'eng-lai have completely dried up. What seemed
to him a short visit to the fairy island had been an eon in
the world of men.

In the next poem we have an almost classical cluster of
images associated with the seaways to the east:

> Over the sea, peach flowers have opened on a thousand trees;
> Once Miss Hemp has gone away, none knows when she will
>   come again.
> That old crane from Liaotung must be torpid and lazy:
> They told him to explore the Mulberry Plantation—but then
>   he did not return. (46)

Which is to say: The millennial opening of the peach blossoms of the holy seamount heralds the onset of cosmic spring; Miss Hemp will surely remain there for a long time, savoring scent and spectacle. An aged crane, preparing to return to his northeastern wetlands for the summer, is urged to fly over the dry seabed to P'eng-lai to look for her—but he searched in vain, or perhaps succumbed to the wonders of the place and, rejuvenated, to the beauty of the ever-youthful goddess.

This low road (or high road, if the crane route were elected) was taken regularly by other distinguished ladies. Ts'ao T'ang reports the preparations at P'eng-lai for the arrival of the Royal Mother of the West:

> Jade syrinx and gold zither emit the tone of *shang*:
> The mulberry leaves wither and dry as the sea water clears.
> They sweep the road below Mount P'eng-lai clean,
> Planning to invite the Royal Mother to chat about long life. (1)

The tone of *shang* was, in T'ang times, the foundation of a myxolydian mode.[120] It was also the cosmic note of autumn and the setting sun, the sombre and chilling sound of death emanating from the holy mountain K'un-lun, which dominates the icy western world. The divine orchestra of the Royal Mother's palace has sounded the doom of all living things. Even the sacred mulberries of the East—the fruit that nourishes the immortal beings of the sunrise—are afflicted by this ultimate frost, and as they fade, the waters of the ocean begin to wash over them once more. Concerned by this *memento mori*, the visible evidence of corruption, even the radiant beings of P'eng-lai are troubled, and they quickly prepare special access for the Queen of the West so she may give them new wisdom and training in the arts of longevity. This rather solemn allegory of slow change and decline is quite unlike most of Ts'ao T'ang's lighthearted confections, except insofar as it attributes to these fragile "transcendents" a very human frailty.

In still another quatrain about the Eastern Sea—here called "East Stygia," suggesting its dark remoteness[121]— the treatment of these themes is rather more frivolous:

> East Stygia on two occasions has seen the dust fly,
> And since a myriad years ago such interviews have been rare:
> Now a hundred pots of wine, and the pear blossoms on a
>   thousand trees,
> Unite these lords in argument and drink—but no one will
>   discuss poetry. (89)

Here, then, old friends, separated through two geological eons, meet in the eternal springtime to savor the white vernal flowers, the new wine, and perhaps love. The "pear blossoms" represent mulberries and their millennial burgeoning, and, more remotely, allude to "Pear Blossom Spring" (*li hua ch'un*), the name of a wine which is ready to drink at the time of the flowering of the pear trees in early spring.

Other flowering trees, too, assumed the role of punctuating eternity. In the following poem, Ts'ao T'ang substitutes a more mysterious one than those we have already encountered:

> Blue Lad transmits the word, requiring them to come back:
> His report tells that Miss Hemp's "jade stamens" have
>   opened.
> The Watchet Sea has turned to dust—all other affairs may be
>   disregarded:
> They mount dragon and crane and come to observe the
>   flowers. (81).

Here the Lord of the East sends news to the mainland that requires the immediate return of his court to the east: the wonderful flowers of the bird-woman's garden are opening. Once more it is cosmic spring, and the solar power of *yang* rules the world. The company will make swift passage for the flower-watching holiday at P'eng-lai.

The real novelty in this quatrain is the presence of a flowering plant named "jade stamens" (*yü jui*),[122] which adorns the magic garden of the wind-blown seamount. For some writers and readers, perhaps, this beautiful snow-white bloom was altogether an unearthly flower, doubtless crystalline, and fit food for the gods. But it also had a terrestrial identity. It was a rare plant, known only, it seems, to a few rich gardens, especially in the capital of T'ang, although there are occasional reports of it in Sung times. The most celebrated display was in the garden of a Taoist temple, the Belvedere of T'ang's Glory (*T'ang ch'ang kuan*) in the An-yeh Quarter of Ch'ang-an.[123] A wonderful story relates the remarkable flowers to a Taoist goddess or (to be more precise) a Jade Woman. It tells how the jewel-like deity descended into the temple garden, gathered a few of the flowers—whose spirit she was—and disappeared into the sky, attended by the crunkling of cranes and the shimmer of phosphoric beings. The full tale survives in the version of the ninth-century writer K'ang P'ien[124] but has also merited poetic treatment by Yen Hsiu-fu, Yüan Chen, Liu Yü-hsi, and Po Chü-i.[125] The identity of this rare bloom exercised the detective faculties of some Sung literati. Chou Pi-ta, for instance, reports that he obtained a specimen from the vicinity of Nanking. He provides a good description of the plant and its fantastic flowers, with their "whiskers like threads of ice, with

golden grains sewn on top." It was a climbing shrub, with
ovate leaves, and its flowers were distinguished by a radial
fringe of stamen-like threads, distinct from the stamens
proper. The thready fringe surrounded a central tubular
stalk. These characteristics make its identification possible. It appears to have been a species of passion-flower
vine, or maypop, which is noted for the handsome corona
of filaments that surrounds a central bisexual cylinder
called a gynophore.[126]

Secrets of the solar track,
Sparks of the supersolar blaze.

R. W. EMERSON
"Merlin"

Fu-sang

COMPARED WITH the reasonably accessible seamount of P'eng-lai, the other realms of the Eastern Sea were beyond search or even ordinary understanding. One of these was the hidden world of Fu-sang. The ancient myths that tell of this place, the turbulent womb of the daily renewed sun, have been thoroughly studied and reported in sinological literature, and need no special comment here. A myth of our own times—a charmingly innocent one—identifies this boiling Phlegethon beyond the horizon with North America. But the medieval Taoist picture of that realm has been little advertised.

The name Fu-sang appears to mean, approximately, "Luxuriant Mulberries," a not improbable interpretation in view of the omnipresence of mulberries in the lore of the eastern seas.[127]

To reach this strange place, one must traverse the Stygian Sea (*ming hai*) and its gigantic waves to a distant shore and then proceed overland for an undetermined distance until one reaches the Cyan Sea (*pi hai*), coming finally to the palace of a mighty king, hard by the Valley of Thermae (*t'ang ku*), which lies 60,000 *li* northeast of Fang-chu.[128] This is the ancient bathhouse of the sun, from which that fiery entity emerges each morning renewed.[129]

Fu-sang is a richly forested land, and its soil is pebbled with lumps of jade and of purple gold.[130] The palace of its ruler is called, in the Mao Shan tradition, Palace of the Clarified Prime (*Ch'ing yüan kung*).[131] Its lord rejoices in the title of Supreme Tao Lord, Great Thearch of the Cinnabar Forest in Fu-sang of the Eastern Aurora and Grand Subtlety (*T'ai wei tung hsia Fu-sang tan lin ta ti shang tao chün*).[132] The imagery imbedded in this distinction is closely related to the worshipful aspects of the sun as a concentration of life-giving energy which lifts itself each morning from its secret subterranean chamber, refreshed and renewed. "Cinnabar" is the red mineral essential to all elixirs of life; "aurora" is the pattern of pink rays that herald the rise of the celestial dynamo, and is itself a source of energy. The element "Grand Subtlety" in the god's title suggests a connection with an equatorial sky palace, the Palace of Grand Tenuity (*T'ai wei kung*), which stands at the autumnal equinox, its precincts spread over parts of our constellations Leo, Virgo, and Coma Berenices.[133] This was a southern counterpart of the great Palace of Purple Tenuity at the North Pole. One of the lord's known deeds was the transmission of part of the arcana of Eastern Florescence—that is, from his own archives—to the Lady of Southern Marchmount (Nan Yüeh fu-jen), and through her to the deserving part of mankind.[134]

This remote and noble being is a transformation of that classical but undistinguished personage invented long before to achieve metaphysical balance with the Royal Mother of the West. This was the Royal Father of the East (Tung Wang Fu or Tung Wang Kung). Under Taoist auspices, this "father," formed beyond the Cyan Sea from the Pneuma of Eastern Florescence as an embodiment of the *yang* energy, acquired some conspicuous dynamic qualities but no distinct personality.[135] He survives best in the attractive image of Blue Lad, but is officially embodied in the austere figure of the Lord of Fu-sang. He himself, the progenitor of these handsome personalities, disappeared from religion after Han times, and barely survived in literary folklore.[136]

The Lord of Fu-sang, as the alter ego of the Royal Father of the East, necessarily has a deep, polarized relationship with the Royal Mother of the West, although it is a more formal one than the poetic alliance between that lady and Blue Lad. Lacking anything like the radiant and recognizable personality of his iconographic alter ego, Blue Lad, the Lord of Fu-sang might seem a rather unlikely actor to be cast in the role of lover. Nonetheless, Ts'ao T'ang has managed to portray him successfully as a beloved teacher in this poem of very human sorrow at separation:

When he newly conferred the stanzas of the Eight Immaculates in golden script,

> The Jade Resplendent One instructed me, his handmaiden, to
> become mistress of Fu-sang.
> It has been three thousand years since I was parted from my
> lord;
> Now I actually loathe the length of the days and months in the
> homes of the transcendents. (95)

The situation here is the transmission of a holy scripture
from the heights of heaven down through a hierarchical
chain, ultimately to be revealed to mankind. This is the
"Stanzas of the Eight Immaculates" (*Pa su chang*),[137] a cru-
cial text for the Taoists of the Highest Clarity persuasion,
which reveals the techniques for absorbing solar and lunar
essences. It originates with the supreme deity, called Jade
Resplendent (*yü huang*). This high personage directs one of
his jade maidens to carry the sacred scroll down to the Fu-
sang Palace, and to take up residence there as bride and
preceptress of its master. (Later this mighty king passed the
scripture on to the Royal Mother of the West, who in turn
conferred it on the inspired youth Yang Hsi, the ultimate
fountainhead of the Mao Shan tradition.) Now several mil-
lennia have passed since the lady completed her mission and
returned to the court above the stars. But she has never
forgotten her self-fulfilling task, and gets little joy out of
her immortality. The slow, uneventful pulse of the cosmic
clock oppresses her—even the quick, passionate careers of
mortal men would be preferable.

The deity who personifies the newborn sun had a special
need for the presence of his metaphysical rival and occasional partner, most especially on great ceremonial occa-
sions. The Great Yin was required to provide equipoise
with the Great Yang. At such times the condensing and
conserving feminine presence restored the cosmic har-

mony. Such is the dominant image of Ts'ao T'ang's picture of a mysterious and haunting reception:

> The season when the Prior Born of Sunbath Valley comes
>   down to the feast:
> The moonlight has first cooled the purple snow-gem's
>   branches.
> Keen and clear [sounds of] metal and stone shoot up from
>   heaven and earth;
> The matter is an affair of our world, yet no man is aware [of
>   it]. (39)[138]

"Purple snow-gem" (*tzu ch'iung*) seems to be a reflex of the name of the tree *Callicarpa dichotoma* of central and southern China, called "purple bead" (*tzu chu*) because of its handsome clusters of purple berries. Here we have to do with a celestial counterpart of that tree—with amethystine berries. "Metal and stone" is a common synecdoche for bronze bells and lithophones, the dominant musical instruments in medieval religious rites. Their sounds are projected throughout the cosmos.

The locus of this rite is not made clear, but it seems likely that the sun god is visiting the temporal world at its western extremity, where the physical sun sets. It is midnight; the full moon shines on a sacred grove in K'un-lun. Sacred music rings through the aether to welcome him. Elsewhere on earth, this event is known, if at all, only to Taoist initiates. An encounter between the Great Thearch of the Cinnabar Forest and the Royal Mother of the West necessarily had an elevated sacred character—no idle flirtation was possible. The responsibility for more tender relationships, on the fringes of the human world, was left to the more approachable figure of Blue Lad.

What was the ointment sprinkled on my beard?
What were the hymns that buzzed beside my
     ear?
What was the sea whose tide swept through me
     there?
Out of my mind the golden ointment rained,
And my ears made the blowing hymns they
     heard.
I was myself the compass of that sea.

WALLACE STEVENS
"Tea at the Palaz of Hoon"

Blue Lad and the Fang-Chu Palace

NOT SO MYSTERIOUS as Fu-sang, but equally inaccessible, was the home of an important divinity commonly styled Blue Lad (*Ch'ing t'ung*). Long an important personage in the Mao Shan pantheon,[139] he figures repeatedly in T'ang literature at every level, from solemn invocations to the half-serious frivolities of Ts'ao T'ang. His blue color has to do with his eastern associations. The symbolic color of the east is green—the color of new vegetation, associated with the season of spring and the rain-bringing dragon. But the ancient word for the color of verdure once covered the whole blue-green part of the spectrum. In medieval times it had come to mean chiefly "blue," and was understood in the sense of "green" only when applied to growing plants—a convention that puzzled the Chinese themselves.[140] Blue Lad's characteristic garment was a "draconic stole of volant blue halcyon plumage."[141] Still, when Li Po saw him in a vision, he reported that his hair was unambiguously green.[142] At any rate, he was the god of fertility, generation, rebirth, and optimistic life. In consequence, he loomed importantly in the literature of Highest Clarity, in which persuasion his full and resonant title is "The Lord, Small Lad of Blue Florescence, King of the Eastern Sea, High Master of the Dawn, Great Supervisor of Destinies, Superior Minister at the Golden Pylons, Jade Conservator-King, the Grand Realized One of the Nine Subtleties."[143] (Some of these epithets give him a messianic status, as judge of the worth of persons for immortality and the supernal life.)

Blue Lad's magic palace is called Fang-chu Palace (*Fang-chu kung*). Its secret repository is the Archive of the Blue Prime (*Ch'ing yüan fu*).[144] *Fang-chu* is an old word whose etymology has been long disputed.[145] Essentially it was the name of a dish for collecting dew fallen from the humid surface of the moon. It was said to have been made of copper in ancient times, or of a fusion of minerals. Sometimes it had the form of a mirror. But although often a kind of alchemical artifact, it might even be a large clamshell. As a magical moon-dew mirror, its associations were with midnight rituals and the power of *yin*. In T'ang times, at least, pharmacologists still advocated the collection of moon-dew on the night of the second new moon of autumn, to be ingested for the banishment of hunger and the prolongation of life.[146] But it is not obvious why the seamount (if such it was—at least it was a mountain overseas) should have the name of a magic moon-mirror. One explanation could be that as the residence of the dawn-lord of life-giving *yang*, it must continue to maintain its balance with the energy of *yin*, just as in traditional symbolism the figure of the lusty hare lurks in the core of the moon, that great pool of *yin*, and contrariwise a dark crow inhabits the depths of the sun, that shining reservoir of *yang*. It may also be relevant that the *Chen kao* declares that the court-iers of Blue Lad, although they have in fact achieved the Tao, continue to maintain perfect somatic harmony by dosing themselves regularly with the potent rays of both sun and moon.[147]

But the lunar associations of Blue Lad, an important member of the *dramatis personae* in Ts'ao T'ang's "Saun-ters in Sylphdom," are insignificant in the poet's little masques. The moon appears at his celestial feasts only in its utilitarian aspect, as it does in the terrestrial rituals which mimic the exalted pageants of the gods. Such appears to be the case in a quatrain in which Blue Lad appears under his title of Lord of the Nine Solarities (*Chiu yang chün*), that is, as master of all cosmic manifestations of *yang*:

> The green park and its pink halls are pressed under auspicious clouds;
> The moon illuminates a holiday feast for the Lord of Nine Solarities.
> No one knows who was drunk first last night:
> Daylight shatters the luminous auroras—an eight-zoned skirt!
> (88)[148]

Here the full moon illuminates a midnight fete in a celestial garden—as the Grand Yin it is an appropriate lamp, but it seems to have nothing special to do with Blue Lad, who evidently has enjoyed a private assignation and carouse with an unnamed lady. The bright light of day brings these affairs to a close, shredding the pink film in the eastern sky as if it was the lady's thin skirt. This image is not uncommon. Another poet of the T'ang once characterized the fine auroral fabric as cut into strips by the scissors of the wind "to make a dress for a transcendent person,"[149] and Ts'ao T'ang himself has written elsewhere of the "skirt of halcyon and aurora" worn by the sister of Blue Lad.[150]

The moon appears again in another setting by Ts'ao T'ang, where Blue Lad is shown searching for another solar divinity:

> The wine exhausted, the incense wasted away—the night wills its own midpoint;
> Blue Lad salutes—asks after the Lord of Purple Solarity.
> The light of the moon is soft and still—syrinx and song recede;
> The silhouettes of horses, the sounds of dragons—they are homeward bound through the Five Clouds. (41)

The Lord of Purple Solarity (*Tzu yang chün*) was, in his mortal condition, Chou I-shan, an archaic and most venerated divinity in the Mao Shan lineage. He is now established as ruler of the Grotto-Heaven of the Golden Altar beneath the roots of Mao Shan itself. In Ts'ao T'ang's poem he has been attending a party, lit by some avatar of the moon; but as midnight approaches he vanishes, leaving his colleague, the Lord of the Fang-chu Palace, behind. The sacred panpipes and holy songs of his cortege fade into the moonlit sky: the creatures who draw his carriages are already only shadows and echoes beyond the auspiciously tinted mists that whirl around the celestial garden.

And where is the mysterious Fang-chu Palace and its
island or mountains? Since its atmosphere is more unearthly than that of P'eng-lai, we have the impression that it is
much farther away. Most sources provide little evidence,
but the *Chen kao*[151] states confidently that it lies 70,000
li southeast of Kuai-chi, that is, from the coast of Chekiang.[152] In the following dream of the ocean isles by
Ts'ao T'ang, the distance is linguistically much shorter than
that—but the number is purely symbolic and easy to
manage:

> She would like to detain her lord—give him Cinnamon Syrup;
> Through the Nine Heavens there is nothing ado—no menaces
>   for him to dispose of.
> His blue dragon lifts its feet, to travel a thousand *li*;
> Don't tell it that the home-road to P'eng-lai is long! (55)

This little tale may be paraphrased as follows: A lovely
lady is loath to let her divine lover depart, urging that his
magic power over cosmic disorders is not, for the nonce, in
need. But he leaves on the long journey anyhow—only a
short canter to his scaly steed. There seems to be little
doubt that "her lord" is Blue Lad, in view of the color of
his dragon-horse, and his home over the dire, dawnward
sea. Indeed, in these poems P'eng-lai is as much his home
as Fang-chu—perhaps more so. The latter appears to be
his private sanctum, the former his country house, where
he entertains the Royal Mother of the West—although on
this occasion it is she who has been entertaining him. The
"cinnamon syrup" that she offers him, as a special treat,
is known to early mythology. In the book of the "Nine
Songs," the protagonist drinks that invigorating beverage
from the starry Dipper. In a later tale the same nectar is the

common drink of the inhabitants of an unknown land, who dress in feathers and abstain from cereals; they are so tenuous that they cast no shadows—in short they are sylphine transcendents.[153] In effect, the lady has tried to retain Blue Lad by offering him the celestial equivalent of a rare bottle of Château Yquem or Johannisberger Riesling—for mortals a life-prolonging elixir. (This poem also embodies the characteristically Taoist motif of the shrinking of space—and therefore also of the time needed for the flight home.)

Turning back to the *Chen kao* again, that book provides a fairly detailed description of the Fang-chu mountain-palace. It is 1,300 *li* along each of its four sides, and it is 90,000 feet high. This massif is in turn adorned with other prominences, such as the Ever-Luminous Grand Mountain and the High Mound of the Night Moon.[154] (Here too we find lunar associations.) Everywhere the vegetation is lush and the fruits are rich, the flowers splendid: many if not all of the forms of plant life, and the waters of the rivers, are tonic and regenerative, and tend to augment vitality. The private palace of the Blue Lord, 200 *li* square, stands on the Mountain of Eastern Florescence (*Tung hua shan*). The halls and towers of this great complex are made of the most precious stones and metals: "rose-gem and azure-gem intermingled make their beams and eaves." The Blue Palace of Fang-chu is planted with hundreds of jade trees, and is supplied with delightful and useful things: royal mews stocked with fighting cocks and phoenixes, mushroom plantations, and a well providing water that rewards its drinker with life as durable as the sun, moon, and stars.[155] Within the palace grounds are the various private residences of Blue Lad, such as the Yellow Chamber in the

Cinnabar Watchtower (*tan ch'üeh huang fang*) and the
House of the Dark Sapphire Depths of Space (*lin hsiao
shih*) at the Watchtower of Phosphors in the Clouds (*yün
ching ch'üeh*).[156] His carriages are equally magnificent:
when he comes to his blue mountain house he travels in a
landau carved from jade, drawn by orbicular concretions of
pneumas.[157]

An important Highest Clarity scripture, a large part of
which is devoted to the realm of Blue Lad, provides other
details. The palace has six gates, each for the use of different
beings. For instance, the western gate, called Gate of the
Jade Grotto, is for the convenience of the Royal Mother of
the West, obviously a regular visitor. All are guarded by
lions. Within are three "Blue Palace" enclosures, of which
Fang-chu is the first. This divine close is planted with jade
trees in which numinous birds roost; magical plants bloom
all about, and magical animals disport themselves among
them. The tablets of life, which display the names of those
mortals who have achieved the boon of transcendence, are
displayed there. Everywhere throngs of sylphine beings
and jade women conduct their tranquil lives.[158]

According to the *Chen kao*, Fang-chu, like P'eng-lai, is
triune. Two lesser mountains—but grand by ordinary
standards—stand to east and west of the central one, each
at a distance of 3,000 *li*. Like the chief residence of the lord
of that land, they are adorned with palatial buildings, and
support all kinds of wonderful plants and animals. The
westernmost of the three mountains is unique: it is inhabited by a great community of Buddhists, who live forever
because they feast on herbs of immortality. There is no
evidence that they desire to escape into nirvana.

The rest of the Blue Lord's domain is populated by
recognizably Taoist personages, and his court and admin-

istration are composed of "celestial transcendents" and "high realized ones." His exalted viziers and stewards are divinities of the Grand Culmen (*t'ai chi*) and Supervisors of Destiny (*Szu ming*). The names of some of these excellent beings are known in our world. Among his ministers is a certain Lord Yang; his younger sister Ch'un Wen-ch'i is styled "Jade Consort" (*yü fei*); there is also the jade woman Yen Ching-chu, and an anonymous attendant, the tutelary deity of White Stone Mountain, where, in his earthly existence, he had become a master alchemist.[159] Otherwise this happy land maintains a blameless population of transcendent beings, who subsist on a diet of the red mulberries that mature once each thousand years, in phase with the ebb and flow of the vast tides that cover the Mulberry Fields.[160] This food imbues their bodies with a beautiful golden color, and gives them the power to fly freely through space.[161]

The inhabitants of eastern Fang-chu, all presumably of the class of Middle Transcendents, have their own special attributes. They live among rare gems and other treasures, notably the "celestial treasures" (*t'ien pao*) of Blue Lad himself, which are kept in storage there. They dine on such marvelous local products as "white jade wine," and a "golden syrup" which spurts out of a rock. These noble beverages impart a golden sheen to their bodies, too. They are excellent musicians, and can be heard performing on their great syrinxes from a distance of 40 *li*. It is said that these concerts, like recitals of Orpheus, attract wild animals of every sort, who dance to their melodies, while divine birds approach and sing in harmony with them. Ranked below the excellent beings are hosts of "Lads of the Jade Dawn" (*yü ch'en chih t'ung*) and "Lads of the Purple Dawn" (*tzu ch'en chih t'ung*), all projections of Blue Lad himself.[162]

But these personages hardly figure in Ts'ao T'ang's poetical world. Although occasionally peers and gentry may be distinguished and maidservants and footmen recognized, only one figure really counts: the noble image of Blue Lad—when he can be identified with certainty. Indeed that is part of the game: is the mysterious milord really Blue Lad at all, or someone wearing his false-face, or some chance look-alike?

What is the game? It is the game of celestial love, oscillating between the follies of courtly intrigue and the eternal verities. It is an allegory of the shiftings and interpenetrations of *yin* and *yang*. Blue Lad—or some plausible replica of him—is always the suitor. He is the attractive male *sub specie aeternitatis*. He is, in fact, a civilized fertility god. This doubtless explains why he figures in light literature as a divine lover. Jade maidens and female neophytes yearn for him—as do even more exalted creatures. His realm of Eastern Florescence (*tung hua*) matches the Western Florescence (*hsi hua*) of the Royal Mother of the West. They appear together regularly engaged in some sort of platonic courtship. Often they are incognito or masked. In any case their flirtations represent the divine interaction of *yin* and *yang*, shown as a colorful union in a glittering environment, rather than an abstract fusion of principles.

Here Ts'ao T'ang presents the ever-youthful deity as an unreliable lover:

> The time when the Numinous Youth of the Cyan Sea came by night—
> She labored in vain to call him up to the Rose-Gem Lake.
> But, since he is not second to the Son of Heaven in his ability at "idle affairs,"
> Even though she gave him a blue dragon he didn't know how to mount it. (54)

To paraphrase: The magical ruler of the dawn once visited K'un-lun, where its queen tried to lure him into her secret garden. He, however, as frail as the Tranquil Son of Heaven long ago, preferred to carouse with boon companions and became so drunk that he could not even mount his own steed.

Indeed, Blue Lad is normally represented by Ts'ao T'ang as quite a lad—a kind of cosmic playboy, but always a perfect gentleman. He is very closely related to Liu Ch'en and Juan Chao, the sometime lovers of jade women in the recesses of Mount T'ien T'ai—the dream lovers of aspiring Taoist priestesses—and to those other semidivine worthies, the Martial Thearch of Han, the Tranquil Son of Heaven, Wang Tzu-ch'iao, Hsiao Shih, and the other reluctant heroes or lucky demigods.[163]

Thus it is not always easy to identify the protagonist of Ts'ao T'ang's little romances. I have singled Blue Lad out for special attention in this essay, but Hsiao Shih and the others have their own poetic settings—and in many quatrains these personages merge with each other to produce hybrid or indeterminate images. Even the powerful figure of Blue Lad often quivers and trembles, and takes on some attributes of other glamorous divinities. Ts'ao T'ang's illusions are unstable, and the personalities of his actors are elusive or even protean.

> The palace watchtowers, doubled and redoubled, shut out the
>   jade forest;
> On the high ramparts of K'un-lun, painted clouds deepen.
> A yellow dragon wags its tail, enticing the Esquire away;
> She sends a maidservant to look for him everywhere under the
>   light of the moon. (7)

The scene here is the high and heavily fortified fastness of the crystal castle of K'un-lun—the axial palace. The re-

vels are over, the gates are shut, and magical clouds gather
to conceal the holy fortress. A young demigod—the title
"esquire," regularly used of either one of the pair Liu
Ch'en and Juan Chao, has here become a pseudonym of
Blue Lad—prepares to leave on his dragon-steed. But his
sweetheart—doubtless Hsi Wang Mu—sends one of her
jade maidens to look for him, and, if possible, to lure him
back.

Sometimes the male masquerader is disguised in another
way. For instance, there is a quatrain in which the mysterious protagonist is not concealed by distance or an inter-
posed barrier, but by another person's title.

> The eldest daughter of the Resplendent One of the East, of not
>   many years,
> Joins them to go to the riverside to wash golden mushrooms.
> With nothing to do, she pairs off with another in a game of *go*,
> And recklessly games away her money for buying flowers.
>   (70)

Which may be interpreted to mean: A little princess of the
realm of the sunrise goes off with a bevy of young ladies to
clean ambrosial mushrooms. She becomes bored, and, having no real responsibilities, she engages "another" in a
board game, heedlessly losing the money that had been entrusted to her for the purchase of flowers. The identity of
her opponent in the gambling session is a problem, but
probably not an important one; the word suggests another
member of the group of maidens. But the Resplendent One
of the East (*tung huang*), her distinguished father, is
another matter. The title appears at first sight to be an
abbreviation of the title of one of the great direction deities
of the remote Heaven of Jade Clarity—a faceless, nameless
entity, of the type that does not engage in relationships

with humans or even with redeemed humans and is not known to have children, differing in this from both Blue Lad and the Royal Mother.[164] Here it is almost certainly an epithet of Blue Lad himself—*ad hoc* but reasonable.

The situation is more mystifying in the next example, where none of the protagonists is identified, even by a doubtful title, and we have to search for spiritual fingerprints with an iconographic lens. Here we have two players, neither named nor plainly alluded to:

> Last night one invited the other to a party at the Apricot Altar;
> Quite reckless, buoyed by intoxication, one drove a blue simurgh away.
> Pink clouds blocked the road—the east wind pressed hard,
> And blew a lotus crown of cyan jade to shreds. (47)

The scene here is ordinary enough. The host in such romantic situations is normally female—the parting guest male. This indifferent lover must be adjudged to be Blue Lad. He is identified by the color of his bird-vehicle and of his crown. The apricot flowers tell us that it is early spring—the season of idle flirtations and sacred marriages alike. The presence of an altar—that is, a stage for the performance of holy rites—indicates that, however brief the affair, it had aspects of a hierogamy.[165] There is nothing to tell us the name of the lady. The amorous guest, too dazed to navigate efficiently, is fighting his way against the gushes of pink auroral plasmas that emanate from his own cerulean realm across the sea.

But there often is another difficulty which compounds the ambiguity. This is the muffled presence in the poem of a watcher who is neither named, nor otherwise identified, and whose gender is even in doubt. This enigmatic lurker

in the shadows, this mocking masquerader in the shrub-
bery, seems to be the author's persona partially realized
among the *dramatis personae*, through whose eyes we gain
a desired perspective on the action. This veiled personage is
usually not detected until the second couplet of the
poem—often not until the last verse. At this point there
may be a soft, ambiguous voice, or a musical note, or the
whinny of a celestial steed. Who is the speaker, the singer,
the owner of the horse? The reader is puzzled, and com-
pelled to reread the poem, looking for a clue to the invisible being's identity. There is always a clue, if sometimes
a tenuous one. Sometimes there is more than one. It may
be an attribute, or an association, or an action, or an
attitude—but it may and sometimes does lead to the transient or modified identity of the lurking personage.

The following quatrain, which also features a transcendent minx—a sylphine gamine—supplies an example:

> Cranes are not flying eastward, dragons do not move;
> The dew is dried up, the clouds are shattered—a vented syrinx
>   calls clear.
> A sylphling, few in years, talks about idle matters;
> Far off, beyond the painted clouds, she hears the sounds of
>   laughter. (31)

A "vented syrinx" (*tung hsiao*) is a set of panpipes whose
tubes, unlike an ancient variety that was topped with wax,
were open. "Sylphling" is *hsien tzu*, a "transcendent
child," normally female. "Painted clouds" (*ts'ai yün*) show
lucky colors. The sacred cranes remain in China, postponing their spring migration to Liaotung; the rain-dragon is
still torpid. Winter is prolonged. The land is dry, and no
nimbus clouds approach—a divine music has halted the

progress of seasons. A pretty sprite is revealed, chatting of this and that with her friends. Heralded by auspicious auras, a noble suitor approaches, chuckling with confidence. If he is the person who has made time stand still with his piping, it might be Hsiao Shih, he who could charm divine birds with his magic syrinx.[166] But it is not he—or not he altogether. The "painted clouds" symbolize the presence of vernal warmth and fertilizing rain, revealing the glamorous figure of Blue Lad, partly infected with some of the attributes of his occasional stand-in, the bird-charmer Scribe Hsiao.

The mask of the longed-for psychopomp must suit the aspirations and circumstances that require his presence.

How much of it was light and how much
    thought,
In these Elysia, these origins,
This single place in which we are and stay,
Except for the images we make of it,
And for it, and by which we think the way,
And being unhappy, talk of happiness...

WALLACE STEVENS
"*Extracts from Addresses to the Academy of Fine
    Ideas*"[167]

Notes

INTRODUCTION

1. CTS, han 12, ts'e 1; CTW, 924, *passim*; Kroll, 1978, 16–30; Kroll, 1981, 19–22.

2. CTS, han 3, ts'e 4–6; CTW, 347–350, *passim*; Waley, 1950; Schafer, 1977a, 123–125; Schafer, 1978c, 5, 15.

3. CTS, han 12, ts'e 6; CTW, 925–926, *passim*; Schafer, 1981, *passim*; Schafer, 1983a, *passim*.

4. CTS, han 3, ts'e 2; CTW, 336–344, *passim*; Schafer, 1977b, *passim*.

5. CTS, han 4, ts'e 9; CTW, 528–530, *passim*; Schafer, 1980b, 50–51.

6. CTS, han 5, ts'e 7; CTW, 623, 15b–16a.

7. CTS, han 11, ts'e 10; Schafer, 1977a, 181.

8. CTS, han 8, ts'e 8; CTW, 760, 24a–24b; Schafer, 1980b, 51.

9. CTS, han 9, ts'e 2.

10. CTS, han 11, ts'e 10.

11. CTS, han 9, ts'e 10; CTW, 800–802, *passim*; Schafer, 1980b, 52.

12. CTS, han 9, ts'e 9; CTW, 796–799, *passim*.

13. CTS, han 12, ts'e 6; CTW, 929–944, *passim*; Schafer, 1979, 31–42, especially 32.

14. See Schafer, 1978a, *passim*.

15. Schafer, 1980a, 92–99.

16. For his poems, see CTS, han 11, ts'e 5.

17. For his poems, see CTS, han 11, ts'e 5; CTW, 891, 6b–7b.

18. Schafer, 1967, 83–86.

19. Schafer, 1982b, 102–124.

20. In the section "Taoist Poets of T'ang."

21. Schafer, 1979, 31–32.

22. The number supplied parenthetically after each translation of a Ts'ao T'ang quatrain refers to its position in the sequence of CTS.

23. Schafer, 1981, 400–401, n. 91.

24. The word here translated "wallet" was a small pouch, such as that worn by officers of the T'ang court, attached to the belt with a gold-inlaid belthook.

25. Schafer, 1977a, 55.

26. *Ibid.*, 6.

27. Schafer, 1967, 8.

28. Schafer, 1977a, 6; Schafer, 1981, 393, n. 66. In the second of these sources I observed, with regard to Wu Yün's astral cruises: "It is generally becoming apparent that Wu Yün's vision is not only of the transit of outer space, but of a mystical journey through the adept's own body." The reader may be able to visualize aspects of such a journey by recalling the film "Fantastic Voyage" (1966), in which a miniaturized boat with a crew of surgeons passes through a series of organs in their patient's body.

29. Schafer, 1967, 119.

30. Schafer, 1977a, 26.

31. PHC, 104.

32. Carl Chun, a German teuthologist, describing the luminescent deep-sea squid, as quoted by Frank W. Lane, "The Home Life of the Octopus," *Saturday Book*, No. 23 (1963), 221–222. The reader may wish to compare this passage with a Taoist description of the jeweled body of a goddess of Highest Clarity in Schafer, 1977a, 233.

33. I Corinthians, 15 : 40.

34. *Ibid.*, 15 : 53.

35. The familiar translation "emperor" is quite misleading. *Ti* represents a divine or numinous being; neither the Roman military title *imperator* nor the later connotation of an emperor as the superior of kings is appropriate to the Chinese concept. Many legitimate "thearchs" ruled tiny nations, without invalidating the meaning of their title.

36. Schafer, 1963, 210.

37. Schafer, 1981, 402, n. 98.

38. Schafer, 1977a, 65.

39. John Addington Symonds, "In the Key of Blue" (1893).

40. Schafer, 1981, 398, n. 81.

41. Schafer, 1967, 158.

42. Schafer, 1977a, 4–5.

PART ONE

1. WTSP, 1, 6a–6b, makes it Liu-chou, whose administrative seat was about ninety miles southwest of that of Kuei-chou. TSCS, 58, 16b–17b, and TTTC, 230–231, apparently based on the preceding, make it Kuei-chou.

2. WTSP.

3. TTTC.

4. *Ibid.*

5. See below, the section "Mythical Heroes," for their story.

6. WTSP. In this version the ladies identify the lodging as the place

alluded to in the second couplet of the fourth of Ts'ao T'ang's five poems about Liu and Juan. The language differs slighty from other versions of the incident in beginning with the words "Below the trees," where TSCS has "Below the water" and TTTS has "Within the grotto." The last of these is the wording favored by CTS, and indeed Ts'ao T'ang seems fond of the phrase "within the grotto," which occurs at the beginning of three of his "Hsiao yu hsien shih" (Nos. 18, 32, and 87), and seems well suited to the tale of the two favored lads at the Peach Flower Grotto. WTSP cites another anecdote prophetic of Ts'ao T'ang's death: the story goes that the poet once said of Lo Yin's poem "Verses on a Peony" (*T'i mu-tan* 題牡丹), that the flower was represented as a courtesan—a beautiful but cold woman with the art of moving men. To this Lo Yin retorted that the two lines of Ts'ao T'ang's poem, to which all of these anecdotes refer, must tell about a ghost—that is, his friend was writing about his own imminent death. In the version of the CTS the couplet reads:

> Within the grotto there is a sky—but spring there is bleak and forlorn;
> There is no road from among men, and the moon fades in a blue infinity.

(To paraphrase, the fairy maidens in their underground paradise are desolate because they are cut off forever from their human lovers: their time scales can never be reconciled. This is one of Ts'ao T'ang's favorite topics.) In the account of his death in TSCS, the poet writes the couplet by a garden pool in a different Buddhist monastery. Next day, at the same spot, two women dressed in white approach, chanting those very lines. Ts'ao T'ang dies several days later. The version of TTTC alleges that Ts'ao T'ang had become increasingly melancholy, and that this mood was expressed in his poem on a sick horse. One day he dreamed that a transcendent woman in oriole costume came to him. She wore a flower crown and misty garments. Leaning against a tree, she chanted the same verses about Liu and Juan at T'ien T'ai, and suggested that he go away with her. He awoke, much disturbed, and the next day was taken violently ill and died.

7. WTSP.

8. In CTS, han 10, ts'e 2, ch. 2.

9. There is one more "Yu hsien" poem, detached from the set of ninety-eight. It could well be one of the two missing from the century.

10. Stephen Bokenkamp, after studying the whole of the extant corpus while participating in my seminar on Ts'ao T'ang early in 1983,

decided that many of the poems of han 10, ts'e 2, ch. 1, which treat all of these personages, are in fact remnants of the missing "Greater Saunters in Sylphdom." This opinion was later confirmed when he discovered that a T'ang anthology includes eleven double quatrains classified under the rubric "Greater Saunters in Sylphdom." TTC, 537–540. To these we should probably add the two on Han Wu Ti and Hsi Wang Mu which precede this group in CTS, plus four others imbedded in the group— that is, all seventeen consecutive poems from "Han Wu Ti chiang hou Hsi Wang Mu hsia chiang" (CTS, p. 3827) to "Han Wu Ti szu Li Fu-jen" (CTS, p. 3828).

11.   For the far-reaching implications of this concept, the reader is referred to Wilkins, 1969, 126–129.

12.   Dante Alighieri, *Paradiso*, XXXIII, 145.

13.   Schafer, 1978b, 393.

14.   E.g., in No. 93. See also "Mu Wang yen Wang Mu yü Chiu kuang liu hsia kuan," CTS, han 10, ts'e 2, ch. 1, p. 3b. His legendary adventures are recounted in MTTC and in SIC ch. 3.

15.   E.g., No. 9. See also "Han Wu Ti chiang hou Hsi Wang Mu hsia chiang." CTS, han 10, ts'e 2, ch. 1, pp. 1b–2a and "Han Wu Ti yü kung chung chiang yen Hsi Wang Mu," *ibid.*, p. 2a, and SIC, ch. 5, and above all HWTNC with K. M. Schipper's study of it. Schipper, 1965, *passim.*

16.   SC, ch. 126.

17.   TMC, 1, 1a–1b; Schafer, 1977a, 127.

18.   SC, 28, 0116b; LHC. He appears in No. 56.

20.   E.g., No. 86. LHC; Schafer, 1983c, 372. His full hagiography appears in TPCJTT.

21.   E.g., No. 60. LHC. See also "Hsiao Shih hsi Lung Yü shang sheng," CTS, han 10, ts'e 2, ch. 1, p. 4b.

22.   YML.

23.   E.g., No. 23. See also Ts'ao T'ang's five poems about the youths in CTS, han 10, ts'e 2, ch. 1, pp. 2a–3a. For examples of Taoist priest-esses who yearn for one of the pair, see Schafer, 1978a, 44–45, 46–47, 58.

24.   CLWYT, 18b.

25.   As in No. 20.

26.   Most recently and most completely in Cahill, 1982.

27.   Both appear in HWTNC, as does the royal lady herself. For a more extended account of Hsi Wang Mu's wonderful deeds, composed in T'ang times, see CHL, 1, 9a–10b. The hagiography of Shang Yüan fu-jen appears in the same source at 2, 1a–13b

28.   Schafer, 1978a, *passim.* See especially examples by Wen T'ing-yün 溫庭筠 (p. 36), Lu Ch'ien-i 盧虔虔 (p. 47), and Li Hsün 李珣 (p. 52).

29.   Chimney in a limestone grotto.

30.   An example is a quatrain attributed to an unknown woman of the palace at Lo-yang. It tells of a written message sent out through the drains to be found by any chance passerby. The writer of the poem expresses the wish that in the spring time she too might float out in that manner. T'ien Pao kung jen 天寶宮人, "T'i Lo yüan wu yeh shang," CTS, han 11, ts'e 10, p. 1b.

31.   Fond of chasms and crevices.

32.   Peach blossoms at K'un-lun, at the mouths of grottoes, and close by or far out on the sea appear in Nos. 25, 26, 43, 46, 53, and 99.

33.   Schafer, 1978a, 23–24.

34.   Auden has reminded us of this in a broader sense—as a trait of the literary imagination. W. H. Auden, *The Dyer's Hand and Other Essays* (New York: Vintage Books, 1968), p. 55.

35.   For an excellent example by Szu-k'ung T'u 司空圖, full of gloomy foreboding, see Schafer, 1977a, 190.

36.   The reader is invited to consult Sivin, 1976, 513–526, for an exposition of the profound importance to Taoists of adjusting human time to cosmic time. He takes the particular example of alchemy, whose chief purpose was the enhancement of man's understanding of universal process—such as the tendency of metals in the rocks of the earth to grow towards perfection. The alchemical arts could speed up the slow pace of geological time to accommodate the rapid passage of mortal time. Even the deities practiced a higher form of alchemy; but they were still subject to the wheels of the cosmic clock, however slowly its gears rotated. In some of Ts'ao T'ang's poems the alternation of autumn and spring, much decelerated, is maintained even on the cosmic level; in others, the norm is endless spring. See, e.g., No. 3, translated below, in the section "The Hollow Worlds."

37.   Hassler, 1973, 38.

38.   *Ibid.*, 50.

PART TWO

1.   Soymié, 1956, 141.

2.   SC, 28, 0116b. The story is not new; it has been widely reported in sinological literature.

3.   There is a well-known version in LHC.

4.   SC, 28, 0115a; HS, 25a, 0392a.

5.   HS quoted in TPYL, 38, 8a.

6.   LT, "T'ang wen p'ien" 湯問篇, 5, 19b.

7.   SCC, 5a–5b.

8. SIC, 10, 11b.

9. SCC, 4b.

10. Schafer, 1983a, No. 7.

11. TT, ch. 22, p. 32 (= p. 2890).

12. SS, 20, 2047a.

13. Ch'en T'ao, "Che hsien yin tseng Chao ta shih," CTS, han 11, ts'e 4, ch. 2, p. 5a.

14. *Salsola pestifer*; modern name *tz'u p'eng* 刺蓬.

15. This usage occurs already in ShC, "Wei feng" 衛風, Po hsi 伯兮.

16. SIC, 10, 2a.

17. Li Po, "Sung Chi hsiu ts'ai yu Yüeh" 送紀秀才游越, CTS, han 3, ts'e 5, ch. 16, p. 6b: "So we know that the rocks of P'eng-lai are actually the aigrette of a huge sea-turtle." Elsewhere Li Po wrote: "Don't leave, giant sea-turtle, carrying the three mounts away! [Even] I aspire to walk on the summit of P'eng-lai." Li Po, "Huai hsien ko," CTS, han 3, ts'e 4, ch. 7, p. 5b.

18. CHL, 1, 9a.

19. HSC in TPYL, 676, 5a. This passage does not occur in the modern canon (HY 442).

20. "Refine" (*lien* 鍊 or 煉) refers to the refinement of precious metals by the fiery purging of the dross from the ore.

21. P'i Jih-hsiu, "Ch'u ju T'ai hu," CTS, han 9, ts'e 9, ch. 3, p. 3b.

22. CT, "Hsiao-yao yu."

23. SC, 28, 0115a.

24. SIC, 6, 6a.

25. Wei Ying-wu, "Yung shan-hu," CTS, han 3, ts'e 7, ch. 8, p. 1a.

26. For more on Chinese knowledge of coral, see Schafer, 1963, 246, where there is also a slightly different translation of Wei Ying-wu's quatrain.

27. SCC, 5a.

28. TPYL, 674, 6b.

29. CLWYT, 30a.

30. TPYL, 38, 8b.

31. Schafer, 1970, 113–114.

32. See Santillana and Dechend, 1977, 60–61, where it is suggested that the shape of a double cone represents the figure swept out slowly during the precession of the equinoxes, as the equatorial pole shifts slowly around the stable ecliptical pole.

33. For P'eng-lai as a calabash, see Stein, 1942, 45–58. Stein notes (p. 51) that at the end of Chou P'eng-lai was imaged as a floating gourd, and points out (pp. 53–54) that *hu-lu* (*ghu-lu 葫蘆 = 壺盧) "calabash" is

cognate to *hu-lun* (*hwĕt-lun* 囫圇), *hun-lun* (*ghwĕn-lywin* 渾淪), and *k'un-lun* (*kwĕn-lwĕn* 崑崙) as well as to a separate series, typified by *hun-t'un* (*ghwĕn-dwĕn* 渾沌) the cosmic egg.

34. Schafer, 1983a, No. 21.

35. Li Po, "Ming t'ang fu," CTW, 347, 3b.

36. CS, 114, 5b.

37. *Ying* 影, cognate to *ying* 映 "projected image; reflection," and to *ching* 景 "phosphor."

38. NS, 2, 2551b.

39. See the two T'ang systems of TTKFT (YCCC, 27, 401–410) and TTFTC.

40. See Sivin, 1976, 513–526.

41. Han Yü 韓愈, "Hsin mao nien hsüeh," CTS, han 5, ts'e 10, ch. 5, p. 1a.

42. Schafer, 1977a, 200.

43. A title bestowed on her by Metal Mother (*Chin mu* 金母). YCCC, 101, 14b.

44. CLWYT, 6b.

45. TCYC, quoted in TPYL, 674, 1a.

46. CHKC in CTS, han 7, ts'e 3, ch. 12, pp. 8b–12a; also in TTTS, 583. "Most Great Realized One" was the title of a daughter of the Royal Mother. See the hagiography of T'ai chen fu-jen 太真夫人 in CHL, ch. 4.

47. "Cast-light" translates *ying* 影. "Scarrow" is "*v.i.* to shine faintly, as through clouds" (*Webster's International*, 2nd ed.), representing *meng-lung* 朦朧.

48. Schafer, 1980b, 6, and 56, n. 41.

49. HLC, and comment in Schafer 1978c, 8. For another example of a visit by astral guests, see the appearance of the Five Oldsters in No. 28, translated below.

50. YCCC, 3, 24.

51. PHC, 1042.

52. Schafer, 1977a, 131–137.

53. STCLC (YCCC, 101, 1385).

54. TST (YCCC, 43, 613).

55. CK, in TPYL, 669, 4b.

56. THC, in TPYL, 675, 1b.

57. CHC, in TPYL, 672, 6a.

58. Schafer, 1978b, 396. This technique is quite old in Highest Clarity Taoism.

59. CLWYT, 6b and 7b.

60. CLWYT, 7b, 14b, and 15a.

61.   CLWYT, 14b.

62.   *Ibid.* From their color they would appear to have a special connection with the East, but they appear in many environments. They seem to be related to a mysterious Thearchic Lord of the Blue Waist (*Ch'ing yao ti chün* 青要帝君), propagator of CYC, a fundamental scripture on Blue Lad.

63.   Schafer, 1977a, pp. 136–137.

64.   THC, quoted in WSPY, 22, 15b–16a. The name "Vermilion Palace" goes back to the "Nine Songs" in the *Ch'u tz'u.*

65.   Paul Kroll has pointed out that Blue Lad refers to himself as *yü huang* in a poem addressed to Wei Hua-ts'un 魏華存 (in WSPY, 20, 11b), apparently the earliest occurrence of the title. Moreover, his alter ego, the Royal Father of the East, is called *Yü huang* (quoted in TPKC, 1, 5a). See Kroll, 1984.

66.   See Nos. 23 and 39.

67.   See, e.g., Nos. 1, 44, 52, and 68.

68.   SHC, 9, 3a–4b.

69.   See CLWYT, 11b, and YCCC, 104, 1423.

70.   See Schafer, 1967, 185.

71.   I owe this plausible suggestion to Paul Kroll. For Mao Ying's full title, see CLWYT, 3b.

72.   Fully treated in Kroll, 1981, 30–34.

73.   TPYL, 675, 2b, attributes the passage to CK, giving a composite version of the costume, close to those of HWTNC (see Schipper, 1965, 94) and CHL, 2, 2b, both of which provide her with a Caftan of Red Frost. For more on this matter see Kroll, 1981, 40, n. 53. But the old Highest Clarity Scripture SYC, pp. 38b–39a, invests another goddess with an earlier version of the same costume. SYC's description is of the Yellow Immaculate Primal Mistress (*Huang su yüan chün* 黃素元君), second daughter of the Grand Immaculate Mistress of the Triple Prime (*T'ai su san yüan [yüan] chün* 太素三元[元]君). The Lady of the Highest Prime appears to derive from this triple goddess: she was born of a graphic error, *shang* 上 for *san* 三. For more on this vexed question, see Schipper, 1965, 34, n. 1. In my translation above, "pulsating" represents *hui* 揮 "brandish," which I take to be an error for *hui* 暉 "flashing [light]."

74.   Li Po, "Shang yüan fu-jen," CTS, han 3, ts'e 6, ch. 21, p. 5b.

75.   For gem-cutting diamonds in T'ang, see Schafer, 1963, 221.

76.   *Fata morgana* is the Italian equivalent of Morgan le Fay, sister of Arthur and pupil of Merlin. As a phenomenon of light, it is explained as follows in *Webster's International Dictionary* (2d edition): "1. A fairy

celebrated in medieval tales of chivalry.... 2. In the *Orlando Innamorato* of Boiardo, Fata Morgana appears as a personification of fortune, living at the bottom of a lake. 3. A mirage, esp. one seen at the Strait of Messina, between Calabria and Sicily;—so called because regarded as the work of the fairy of this name." (Morgan is a Welsh name; it has to do with the sea; *cf. mer* as in "mermaid.")

77. LC, "Yüeh ling," commentary; SW.

78. CL, "Hai jen" 醢人.

79. For instance, SS reports that the Chams coat their brick walls with burnt *ch'en* shells. SS, 82, 2533c.

80. Schafer, 1954, 353. See also Schafer, 1967, 207.

81. HNT, "Fan lun hsün" 氾論訓. The text has "The waters generate draconic clam-monsters," or possibly "dragons and clam-monsters," although dictionaries usually prefer the former. The affinity is emphasized by the use of the uncommon graph 蜃 (for *ch'en* 蜃).

82. EYI, 31, 333.

83. PTKM, 43, 58.

84. Liu Hsiao-wei 劉孝威 (?–548), "Hsiao lin hai" 小臨海, CNCPS, p. 1214.

85. For these mermen, who not only wove precious fabrics, but shed pearls for tears, see Schafer, 1963, 80.

86. Chang-sun Tso-fu 長孫佐輔, "Ch'u chou yen kai ku ch'iang wang hai," CTS, han 7, ts'e 9, p. 4a.

87. Chang Hsiao-p'iao 章孝標 (fl. 826), "Sung Chin K'o-chi kuei Hsin-lo," CTS, han 8, ts'e 4, p. 5b.

88. For fuller details see Schafer, 1963, 202–204, Schafer, 1967, 85, and Schafer, 1980a, 27.

89. The *fata morgana* was also sometimes called "markets of the sea" (*hai shih* 海市).

90. Hsü Hun, "Tseng so chih," CTS, han 8, ts'e 8, ch. 9, p. 10b.

91. Schafer, 1970, 79.

92. P'i Jih-hsiu, "Sung Li ming fu chih jen Nan-hai," CTS, han 9, ts'e 9, ch. 7, p. 3a.

93. Ch'ien Ch'i, "Ch'ung sung Lu shih yü shih Jih-pen kuo," CTS, han 4, ts'e 5, ch. 2, p. 14b.

94. P'i Jih-hsiu, "Sung Yüan-tsai shang jen kuei Jih-pen kuo," CTS, han 9, ts'e 9, ch. 7, p. 13b.

95. Li Shang-yin, "Feng t'ung chu kung t'i Ho-chung Jen chung ch'eng hsin ch'uang ho t'ing szu yün chih tso," CTS, han 8, ts'e 9, ch. 3, p. 8b.

96. William Shakespeare, *The Tempest*, act 4, sc. 1, lines 152–156.

97. SC, 27, 0111c.

98. Hsü Ching-tsung (592–672), "Feng ho ch'un jih wang hai," CTS, han 1, ts'e 8, pp. 2a–2b.

99. Wang Wei, "Sung pi shu Ch'ao chien huan Jih-pen kuo," CTS, han 2, ts'e 8, ch. 2, p. 5b.

100. TYTP in TPKC, 237, 7b–8a. For the marvels revealed by Su O, see Schafer, 1963, 37–39.

101. HS, 25a, 0392a.

102. CHL, 5, 15b.

103. Li Shang-yin, "Cheng-chou hsien tsung shu she jen yu," CTS, han 8, ts'e 9, ch. 2, p. 9a.

104. PTSI, in PTKM, 46, 35.

105. Hsü Ning (fl. 813), "Sung Jih-pen shih huan," CTS, han 7, ts'e 10, p. 1b.

106. Ts'ao T'ang, "Wang Yüan yen Ma Ku Ts'ai Ching tse," CTS, han 10, ts'e 2, ch. 1, pp. 3a–3b.

107. The source of this allusion is unknown to me. I find that Hsü Ching-tsung (592–672), "Yu ch'ing tu kuan hsün tao shih te ch'ing tzu," CTS, han 1, ts'e 8, p. 4b, has "Perhaps order the wine of Yü-hang" in a Taoist context. Ts'ao T'ang tells of the Royal Mother ordering it—as from a purveyor to the court by royal appointment—in one of his "Hsiao yu hsien shih" (No. 43). Yü-hang is the chief urban township of Hang-chou.

108. The standard accounts are in SHC: Ma Ku in ch. 7, pp. 1b–2b, Wang Yüan in ch. 2, pp. 2a–3b.

109. SHC, 2, 3a; 7, 2b.

110. SHC, 7, 2a.

111. As beautiful as Venus.

112. Much has been written about this mythological "science." See especially Needham and Wang, 1958, 598–601.

113. Yen Chen-ch'ing, "Fu-chou Nan-ch'eng hsien Ma Ku Shan hsien t'an chi," CTW, 338, 5b–8a. See also Schafer, 1977a, 32. For a brief account of Yen Chen-ch'ing and his work see Schafer, 1977b, 126–129.

114. YTCS, 12, 18b.

115. TTKFT (in YCCC, ch. 27), 404, 406.

116. Ibid., p. 402.

117. For Ting Ling-wei see Schafer, 1983c, pp. 385–396.

118. SHC, 5, 4a–5b.

119. SHC, 8, 1a–1b.

120. Picken, 1981, 27.

121. Tung ming 東溟, the eastern part of the circumambient ocean

(*szu ming* 四溟 or *ming hai* 溟海), elsewhere the Watchet Sea, in which P'eng-lai is situated. See SCC, 5a, and discussion in Schafer 1979, 39, n. 39.

122. *Jui* means, more precisely, the array of sexual organs in the heart of a flower, including both stamens and pistils.

123. The twelfth-century writer Chou Pi-ta notes that there were also specimens at two important government offices of T'ang, on the palace grounds, the Chi hsien yüan 集仙院 and the Han lin yüan 翰林院. See his "Yü jui pien cheng" 玉蕊辨證 in WCC (SKCC), v. 18, ch. 184.

124. CTL (TTTS, 12a–13a; also in TPKC, ch. 69).

125. The poems are given in the CTL. WCC, *loc. cit.*, quotes many other T'ang and Sung writers on the subject of the jade-stamen flower. Some name it "Snow-Gem Flower" (*ch'iung hua* 瓊花). Some thought it to be the same as "Mountain Alum" (*shan fan* 山礬), a tree with fragrant white flowers (*Symplocos prunifolia*). See Stuart, 1911. Li, 1959, favors the view that the *ch'iung hua* was a variety of hydrangea (see pp. 103–108: "The Mysterious Jade Flower"). I have translated Liu Yü-hsi's poem on the Jade-Stamen Flower in Schafer, 1977a, 134.

126. I have found this identification only in F. S. Couvreur, 1963. Other dictionaries are silent. I suspect that the T'ang-Sung garden plant was a cultigen of limited distribution possibly derived from *Passiflora cochinchinensis*, a native of Kwangtung, Kwangsi, and Vietnam, now known as "Vine of the Serpent King" (*she wang t'eng* 蛇王藤). In modern times the vacated name "Jade Stamens" has been reassigned to *Barringtonia* (*Yü jui chu* 玉蕊屬), a genus of tropical trees of the family *Lecythidaceae* (*Yü jui k'o* 玉蕊科).

127. Ts'ao T'ang himself makes this interpretation explicit in a line of verse on an entertainment given by the Tranquil King for the Royal Mother at the "Hostel of Flowing Aurora of Nine Lights": "The mulberry leaves, thickly serried, cover the efflorescence of the sun." "Mu Wang yen Wang Mu yü Chiu kuang liu hsia kuan," CTS, han 10, ts'e 2, ch. 1, p. 3b.

128. This account draws on a number of sources. Among them are CK, 9, 20b–22b; SCC, pp. 1a and 5a.

129. Various cognates of "thermae" substitute for that word in other texts. For instance 暘 *yang* "solar bath," and simple 陽 *yang*. For the basic story, see HNT, ch. 3, referring to *Yao tien* 堯典 (Maspero, 1924, 17). For other variants on the name, see Schafer 1977b, 133, n. 52.

130. SCC, 4b.

131. WSPI, 22, 4b.

132. CLWYT, p. 3b. There are other forms of this title, e.g., *Fu-*

sang t'ai ti chiu lao hsien huang chün 榑桑太帝九老仙皇君 (in YCCC, 8, 97).

133. Schafer, 1977a, p. 52.

134. See HTC, 55, 1b. For more on the Lord of Fu-sang and his bestowal of the Scripture of the Yellow Court, to become the fundamental scripture of Mao Shan Taoism, see Schafer, 1977b, 131, n. 38.

135. CHL, 1, 9a–9b.

136. He is mentioned in ShIC, 1a, and under the title of "Grand Realized Royal Father of the East" is shown residing in the Palace of the Grand Thearch, i.e., of the Lord of Fu-sang, in SCC, *loc. cit.* The title "Grand Thearch" is the special epithet of these eastern monarchs, whether designated as Royal Father or as Lord of Fu-sang. See CLWYT, p. 3b. The title also occurs as the designation of the divinity housed in Polaris (α Ursae minoris), in the form "Heavenly Illustrious Grand Thearch" (*T'ien huang ta ti* 天皇大帝). Schafer, 1977a, 46. Similarly the full title of the Royal Mother of the West contains the phrase "of Purple Subtlety," which links her directly with the polar palace (see, e.g., Ts'ao T'ang's No. 84). These symbolic interconnections represent the balance between great cosmic forces, necessary for ultimate harmony.

137. This is the PSC (HY 1312, and parts of other scriptures). The epithet "in golden script" occurs in the title of a number of sacred texts.

138. Here the Lord of Fu-sang is called "Prior Born" to emphasize both his seniority and his superior wisdom.

139. He was one of the principal deities whose responsibility it was to transmit the Taoist arcana to deserving humans. See Robinet, 1981, I, 178–179. For a more complete account of Blue Lad in his apostolic, hieratic, and hierarchical aspects, see Kroll, 1984.

140. On the ambiguity of *ch'ing* 青 see Schafer, 1982a, 91–92.

141. LSTWC, quoted in TPYL, 675, 5b.

142. I.e., *lü* 綠. Li Po, "Yu T'ai shan, liu shou," No. 3, CTS, han 3, ts'e 6, ch. 19, p. 2b.

143. *Chiu wei t'ai chen yü pao wang chin ch'üeh shang hsiang ta szu ming kao ch'en shih tung hai wang ch'ing hua hsiao t'ung chün* 九微太眞玉保王金闕上相大司命高晨師東海王青華小童君 (CLWYT, 3b). A somewhat different version of this title appears in CTNW, ch. a, p. 1a (probably a work of the fifth century). It is "The Lord, Small Lad of Blue Florescence at the Jade Gate of the Eastern Sea ... [the same] ... The Grand Realized One of Highest Clarity" (*Shang ch'ing t'ai chen yü pao wang shang hsiang ta szu ma ming kao ch'en shih tung hai yü men ... [the same]* 上清太眞玉保王上相大司馬命高晨師東海玉門青華小童君.) The *ma*

of this version appears to be intrusive, but the *yü men* rings truer than the redundant *wang*. In some texts that refer to Blue Lad and his domain we find *"Eastern* Florescence," the name of his mansion on Fang-chu Mountain. (See, for instance, "The Upper Chamber of Eastern Florescence of the Fang-chu Palace" [YCCC, 96, 4b]; Schafer 1983a, 9, n. 28.)

144. WSPY, 22, 4b.

145. A classic description of the place and its inhabitants in CK, 9, 20b–22b, states that the *fang* means "square," referring to the shape of the holy mountain, but does not comment on the meaning of *chu*, which has elsewhere been identified with *chu* 珠 "orb; bead; globe." Squareness certainly accords with the *yin* aspects of the place, since earth/*yin* are ontologically square, as heaven/*yang* are ontologically round.

146. PTSI, in PTKM, 5, 38–39. Specifically the dew was to be collected in a pan, as in antiquity, then reduced by boiling. Ts'ang-ch'i records many wonderful tales about the efficacy of this rare drug.

147. The account of Fang-chu in CK is given as a prelude to the report of the Lady of Southern Marchmount (Nan Yüeh fu-jen 南嶽夫人) on the method employed by the divine beings of Fang-chu in ingesting solar and lunar plasmas. As far as the moon is concerned, she tells that the gullet, which leads down to the red chamber of the heart, is purged by the inhalation of ten white moon rays. CK, 9, 22a. To the Chinese the oscillant night light we call the moon was merely the sensible aspect of the Grand Yin, a partial vision of a kind of storage battery—an actively receptive (rather than merely passive) reservoir of cold, potential energy, the antiphon of the kinetic dynamo of the sun. It is not inert, but the source of its light is latent. For us the moon is merely a mirror illumined by the sun. For them, the moon emits its cool, impassive light when stimulated by the sun, just as a luminescent mineral glows pale blue, or green and white, when stimulated by the "black light" of an ultraviolet lamp.

148. Here I emend an incomprehensible *shu* 書 "write" to *chou* 晝 "day."

149. Wang Chou 王周, "Hsia" 霞, translated in Schafer, 1983b, 24.

150. In No. 20.

151. *Ibid.*

152. Blue Lad had a separate residence on the mainland in Kuai-chi itself. This was in Mount Wei Yü 委羽山, the second of the great grotto-heavens, in the T'ien T'ai region. TTKFT.

153. SIC, 9, 6a.

154. CK, 9, 20b.

155. WSPY, 4, 12b.

156. TCC, quoted in WSPY, 22, 12b.

157. TCC, quoted in TPYL, 674, 3a.

158. CYC, ch. b, pp. 10b–14b. See Robinet, 1981, II, 133–134.

159. CLWYT, 4a, 6b, 7b, 20a.

160. SCC, 4b. The "red" suggests the vitalizing power of *yang*, but the berries of the fully ripe mulberry are dark purple, the polar color. In the T'ang pharmacopoeia, they are reputed to strengthen the soul, increase intelligence, and extend life. TPTC, in PTKM, 36, 73.

161. SCC, 5a; YCCC, 26, 398–399.

162. CTNW, a, 1a and 2a.

163. See above, the section "Mythical Heroes."

164. His full title is *Tung ming kao shang hsü huang tao chün* 東明高上盧皇道君. CLWYT, 1a.

165. The Apricot Altar (*hsing t'an* 杏壇) is sometimes associated with the wonderful healer Tung Feng 董奉 and his grove of apricots. SHC, 6, 6a–6b, but this association seems irrelevant here.

166. LHC, p. 6119.

167. I wish to express particular gratitude to Holly Stevens, who gave me her personal permission to use Wallace Stevens' verses, and showed a gratifying interest in *Mirages on the Sea of Time*.

Bibliographies

PRIMARY SOURCES

Parenthetical abbreviations stand for books listed under "Collectanea, Encyclopedias, and Anthologies." They represent the source or edition used in footnote documentation, unless otherwise stated in the note. Poems reprinted in the CTS are not listed separately in the bibliography; their titles appear, in romanized form, only in the relevant footnotes. However, Taoist books quoted from the *Tao Tsang* or from the Taoist anthology YCCC have individual listings in the bibliography.

CHC	*T'ai i ti chün chen hsüan ching* 太一帝君真玄經 (TPYL)
CHKC	Ch'en Hung 陳鴻 (fl. 813), *Ch'ang hen ko chuan* 長恨歌傳 (CTS; TTTS)
CHL	Tu Kuang-t'ing 杜光庭, *Yung ch'eng chi hsien lu* 墉城集仙錄 (HY 782)
CK	T'ao Hung-ching 陶弘景, *Chen kao* 真誥 (HY 1010)
CL	*Chou li* 周禮
CLWYT	T'ao Hung-ching 陶弘景, *Chen ling wei yeh t'u* 真靈位業圖 (HY 167)
CS	*Chin shu* 晉書 (KM)
CT	*Chuang tzu* 莊子
CTL	*Chü t'an lu* 劇談錄 (TTTS; TPKC)
CTNW	*Shang ch'ing wai kuo fang p'in ch'ing t'ung nei wen* 上清外國放品青童內文 (HY 1362)
CYC	*Ch'ing yao tzu shu chin ken chung ching* 青要紫書金根眾經 (HY 1304)
EYI	Lo Yüan 羅願 (1136–1184), *Erh ya i* 爾雅翼 (TSCC)
HHS	*Hou Han shu* 後漢書 (KM)
HLC	*Pei ti shuo huo lo ch'i yüan ching* 北帝説豁落七元經 (HY 1404)
HNT	*Huai nan tzu* 淮南子
HS	*Han shu* 漢書 (KM)
HSC	*Hou shen tao chün lieh chi* 後聖道君列紀 (TPYL)
HTC	*Huang t'ing nei ching yü ching chu* 黃庭內景玉經注 (HSCC)
HWTNC	*Han Wu Ti nei chuan* 漢武帝內傳 (HY 292)
LC	*Li chi* 禮記
LHC	*Lieh hsien chuan* 列仙傳 (HY 294)
LSTWC	*Ling shu tzu wen ching* 靈書紫文經 (YCCC)
LT	*Lieh tzu* 列子 (*Ch'ung hsü chih te chen ching* 沖虛至德真經) (HY 668)

MTTC   *Mu t'ien tzu chuan* 穆天子傳 (HY 291)

NS   *Nan shih* 南史 (KM)

PHC   *Kao shang yü huang pen hsing chi ching* 高上玉皇本行集經 (HY 10)

PSC   *Pa su ching* 八素經 (HY 1312)

PTKM   Li Shih-chen 李時珍, *Pen ts'ao kang mu* 本草綱目 (A.D. 739) (PTKM)

SC   *Shih chi* 史記 (KM)

SCC   *Hai nei shih chou chi* 海內十洲記 (SK)

ShC   *Shih ching* 詩經

SHC   *Shen hsien chuan* 神仙傳 (SK)

SHCSI   *Shen hsien chuan shih i* 神仙傳拾遺 (TPKC)

ShIC   *Shen i ching* 神異經 (SK)

SIC   *Shih i chi* 拾遺記 (KCIS)

SS   *Sui shu* 隋書 (KM)

STCL   *San t'ien chün lieh chi* 三天君列紀 (YCCC)

SW   *Shuo wen chieh tzu* 說文解字

SYC   *San yüan yü chien pu ching* 三元玉檢布經 (HY 354)

TCC   *Tung chen ching* 洞真經 and *Tao chi ching* 道迹經 (WSPY)

TCYC   T'ao Hung-ching 陶弘景, *Teng chen yin chüeh* 登真隱訣 (TPYL)

THC   *Tao hsüeh chuan* 道學傳 (PTKM)

TMC   *Tung ming chi* 洞冥記 (SK)

TPCJTT Szu-ma Ch'eng-chen 司馬承禎, *Shang ch'ing shih ti ch'en Tung po chen jen t'u tsan* 上清侍帝晨桐栢真人圖譜 (HY 612)

TPTC   *T'ang pen ts'ao chu* 唐本草注 (PTKM)

TSCS   Chi Yu-kung 計有功 (fl. 1135), *T'ang shih chi shih* 唐詩紀事 (SPTK)

TST   *Lao chün ts'un szu t'u* 老君存思圖 (YCCC)

TT   Chu Ch'i-feng 朱起鳳, *Tz'u t'ung* 辭通 (Shanghai, 1934)

TTC   Wei Hu 韋縠 (10th cent.), *Ts'ai t'iao chi* 才調集 (TJHTS)

TTCC   *Ta tung chen ching* 大洞真經 (TPYL)

TTFTC   Tu Kuang-t'ing 杜光廷, *Tung t'ien fu ti yüeh tu ming shan chi* 洞天福地嶽瀆名山記 (HY 599)

TTKFT   Szu-ma Ch'eng-chen 司馬承禎, *T'ien ti kung fu t'u* 天地宮府圖 (YCCC)

TTTC   Hsin Wen-fang 辛文房 (fl. 1304), *T'ang ts'ai tzu chuan* 唐才子傳 (Tokyo, 1972)

TuHC   *Tung hsüan ching* 洞玄經 (WSPY)

TYTP   Su O 蘇鶚, *Tu yang tsa pien* 杜陽雜編 (TPKC)

WCC   Chou Pi-ta 周必大, *Wen chung chi* 文忠集 (SKCC)

WTSP   T'ao Yüeh 陶岳, *Wu tai shih pu* 五代史補 (A.D. 1012) (CKKTP)

YML   *Yu ming lu* 幽明錄 (KHSKC)
YTCS   *Yü ti chi sheng* 輿地紀勝 (1849 ed.)

Collectanea, Encyclopedias, and Anthologies

CKKTP   *Chi ku ko ts'ang pan* 汲古閣藏板
CNPCS   *Ch'üan Han San Kuo Chin Nan Pei Ch'ao shih* 全漢三國晉南北朝詩 (Taipei, 1969)
CTS   *Ch'üan T'ang shih* 全唐詩 (Fu-hsing shu-chü 復興書局, Taipei, 1967)
CTW   *Ch'üan T'ang wen* 全唐文 (Wen-yu shu-tien 文右書店, Taipei, 1972)
HCSS   *Hsiu chen shih shu* 修真十書 (HY 263)
HY   Weng Tu-chien, *Combined Indices to the Authors and Titles of Books in Two Collections of Taoist Literature.* Harvard-Yenching Sinological Index Series No. 25, 1935. Pp. 1–37 enumerate the contents of the *Tao Tsang* 道藏 serially. (My pagination refers to the reprint of the Cheng T'ung version of the canon, published by the I-wen yin-shu-kuan 藝文印書館 at Taipei in 1976.)
KCIS   *Ku chin i shih* 古今逸史
KHSKC   *Ku hsiao shuo kou ch'en* 古小説鈎沈 (*Lu Hsün ch'üan chi* 魯迅全集, Peking, 1973, Vol. 8)
KM   *K'ai ming* 開明 edition
SK   *Shuo k'u* 説庫 (Taipei, 1973)
SKCC   *Ch'in ting szu k'u ch'üan shu shan pen erh chi* 欽定四庫全書善本二集 (Taipei, 1971)
SPTK   *Szu pu ts'ung k'an* 四部叢刊
TJHTS   *T'ang jen hsüan T'ang shih* 唐人選唐詩 (Chung-hua shu-chü 中華書局, Hong Kong, 1958)
TPKC   *T'ai p'ing kuang chi* 太平廣記 (1846 ed.)
TPYL   *T'ai p'ing yü lan* 太平御覽 (*Chung-hua shu-chü* 中華書局 Hong Kong, 1962)
TSCC   *Ts'ung shu chi ch'eng* 叢書集成
TTTS   *T'ang tai ts'ung shu* 唐代叢書 (Taipei, 1968)
WSPY   *Wu shang pi yao* 无上祕要 (HY 1130)
YCCC   *Yün chi ch'i ch'ien* 雲笈七籤 (Tzu-yu ch'u-pan-she 自由出版社 Taipei, 1973)

SECONDARY SOURCES

Cahill, Suzanne E.
1982   *The Image of the Goddess Hsi Wang Mu in Medieval
          Chinese Literature*. (Ph.D. diss., University of California,
          Berkeley, 1982.)
Couvreur, F. S.
1963   *Dictionnaire classique de la langue chinoise*. Book World
          Co., 1963.
Hassler, Donald M.
1973   *Erasmus Darwin*. New York: Twayne Publishers, 1973.
Kroll, Paul W.
1978   "Szu-ma Ch'eng-chen in T'ang Verse." *Bulletin of the Society
          for the Study of Chinese Religions*, 6 (1978), 16–30.
1981   "Notes on Three Taoist Figures of the T'ang Dynasty." *Bul-
          letin of the Society for the Study of Chinese Religions*, 9
          (1981), 19–41.
1984   "In the Halls of Azure Lad." *Journal of the American Orien-
          tal Society*, 105 (1985).
Li, H. L.
1959   *The Garden Flowers of China*. New York, 1959
Maspero, Henri
1924   "Légendes mythologiques dans le Chou King." *Journal
          Asiatique*, 214 (1924), 1–100.
Needham, Joseph, and Wang Ling
1958   *Science and Civilisation in China*. Vol. 3. Cambridge: Cam-
          bridge University Press, 1958.
Picken, Laurence, *et al.*, eds.
1981   *Music from the T'ang Court*. Oxford: Oxford University
          Press, 1981.
Robinet, Isabelle
1981   *La Révélation du Shangqing dans l'histoire du taoisme*. 2 vols.
          Unpublished Thèse de Doctorat d'État, University of Paris,
          1981.
Santillana, Giorgio de, and Hertha von Dechend
1977   *Hamlet's Mill: An Essay on Myth and the Frame of Time*. Bos-
          ton: Godine, 1977.
Schafer, Edward H.
1954   "The History of the Empire of Southern Han according to
          Chapter 65 of the *Wu-tai-shih* of Ou-yang Hsiu." *Silver Jubilee*

Volume of the Zinbun-Kagaku-Kenkyusyo. Kyoto University (Kyoto, 1954), pp. 339–369.

1963 *The Golden Peaches of Samarkand: A Study of T'ang Exotics.* Berkeley and Los Angeles: University of California Press, 1963; reprinted 1981.

1967 *The Vermilion Bird: T'ang Images of the South.* Berkeley and Los Angeles: University of California Press, 1967.

1969 *Shore of Pearls: Hainan Island in Early Times.* Berkeley and London: University of California Press, 1970.

1977a *Pacing the Void: T'ang Approaches to the Stars.* Berkeley, Los Angeles, London: University of California Press, 1977.

1977b "The Restoration of the Shrine of Wei Hua-ts'un at Lin-ch'uan in the Eighth Century." *Journal of Oriental Studies,* 15 (Hong Kong, 1977), 124–137.

1978a "The Capeline Cantos: Verses on the Divine Loves of Taoist Priestesses." *Asiatische Studien,* 32 (1978), 5–65.

1978b "The Jade Woman of Greatest Mystery." *History of Religions,* 17 (1978), 387–398.

1978c "Li Po's Star Power." *Bulletin of the Society for the Study of Chinese Religions,* 6 (1978), 5–15.

1979 "Three Divine Women of South China." *Chinese Literature: Essays, Articles, Reviews,* 1 (1979), 31–42.

1980a *The Divine Woman: Dragon Ladies and Rain Maidens in T'ang Literature.* San Francisco: North Point Press, 1978; reprint of University of California Press publication of 1973.

1980b *Mao Shan in T'ang Times.* Society for the Study of Chinese Religions, Monograph No. 1. Boulder, Colorado, 1980.

1981 "Wu Yün's 'Cantos on Pacing the Void.'" *Harvard Journal of Asiatic Studies,* 41 (1981), 377–415.

1982a "Blue Green Clouds." *Journal of the American Oriental Society,* 102 (1982), 91–92.

1982b "Cantos on 'One Bit of Cloud at Shamanka Mountain.'" *Asiatische Studien,* 36 (1982), 102–124.

1983a "Wu Yün's Stanzas on 'Saunters in Sylphdom.'" *Monumenta Serica,* 33 (1981–1983), 1–37.

1983b "The Grand Aurora." *Chinese Science,* 6 (1983), 21–32.

1983c "The Cranes of Mao Shan." In M. Strickmann, ed., *Tantric and Taoist Studies in Honour of R. A. Stein,* II, 372–393. Mélanges chinois et bouddhiques. Brussels, 1983.

Schipper, K. M.
1965   *L'Empereur Wou des Han dans la légende taoiste: Han wou-ti
       nei-tchouan*. Publications de l'École Française d'Extrême-
       Orient, Vol. 58. Paris, 1965.
Sivin, Nathan
1976   "Chinese Alchemy and the Manipulation of Time." *Isis*, 67
       (1976), 513–526.
Soymié, Michel
1956   "Le Leou-fou chan: Étude de géographie religieuse." *Bulletin de
       l'École Française d'Extrême-Orient*, 48 (1956), 1–139.
Stein, R. A.
1942   "Jardins en miniature d'Extrême-Orient." *Bulletin de l'École
       Française d'Extrême-Orient*, 42 (1942), 1–104.
Stuart, G. A.
1911   *Chinese Materia Medica: The Vegetable Kingdom*. Shanghai,
       1911.
Waley, Arthur
1950   *The Poetry and Career of Li Po, 701–762 A.D.* London: Allen &
       Unwin, and New York: MacMillan, 1950.
Wilkins, Eithne
1969   *The Rose-Garden Game: A Tradition of Beads and Flowers*.
       New York: Herder and Herder, 1969.

Glossaries

The author has made an arbitrary selection of words and names from the text for which he has provided equivalent Chinese "characters" in these glossaries. They do not include expressions whose graphic equivalent should be obvious to a beginning student of Chinese literature, nor those of transient or minimal importance, not requiring supplementation with Chinese characters. (Advanced students will be able to supply these in any case.)

WRITERS

Ch'en Ts'ang-chi 陳藏器
Ch'en T'ao 陳陶
Ch'ien Ch'i 錢起
Chou Pi-ta 周必大
Han Yü 韓愈
Hsü Ching-tsung 許敬宗
Hsü Hun 許渾
Hsü Ning 徐凝
Hsüeh T'ao 薛濤
K'ang P'ien 康駢
Ko Hung 葛洪
Ku K'uang 顧況
Kuo P'u 郭璞
Li Hsün 李珣
Li Po 李白
Li Shang-yin 李商隱
Liu Yü-hsi 劉禹錫
Lo Yin 羅隱
Lu Kuei-meng 陸龜蒙
Ma Tai 馬戴
Ou-yang Chiung 歐陽炯
P'ei Tu 裴度
P'i Jih-hsiu 皮日休
Po Chü-i 白居易
Sung Yü 宋玉
Szu-ma Ch'eng-chen 司馬承禎
T'ao Ch'ien 陶潛
Ts'ao Chih 曹植

Ts'ao T'ang 曹唐
Tu Kuang-t'ing 杜光庭
Tu Mu 杜牧
Wei Ch'ü-mou 韋渠牟
Wei Ying-wu 韋應物
Wu Yün 吳筠
Yen Chen-ch'ing 顏真卿
Yen Hsiu-fu 嚴休復
Yü Hsüan-chi 魚玄機
Yüan Chen 元稹

MYTHOLOGICAL AND DIVINE BEINGS

An-ch'i Sheng 安期生
Chen Yu-hsiao 甄幽蕭
Chia Pao-an 賈保安
Chiang Shu-mao 姜叔茂
Ch'ing T'ung 青童
Chiu T'ien Chen Wang 九天真王
Chiu Yang Chün 九陽君
Chou I-shan 周義山
Hsi Hua Ling Fei 西華靈妃
Hsi Ling Yü Fei 西靈玉妃
Hsi Wang Mu 西王母
Hsiao Shih 蕭史
Hsüan Miao Yü Nü 玄妙玉女
Hu Kung 壺公
Juan Chao 阮肇

143

Kuo Szu-ch'ao 郭四朝
Liu Ch'en 劉晨
Lung-yü 弄玉
Ma Ku 麻姑
Mao Chung 茅衷
Mao Ying 茅盈
Mu T'ien Tzu 穆天子
Nan-yüeh Fu-jen 南嶽夫人
Pi Ch'ang-fang 費長房
Shang Yüan Fu-jen 上元夫人
Su Lin 蘇林
Sung Ch'en-yang 宋晨陽
T'ai Hsüan Shang Hsüan Tan Hsia
   Yü Nü 太玄上玄丹霞玉女
T'ai Hsüan Yü Nü 太玄玉女
T'ai Wei Tung Hsia Fu-sang Tan
   lin Ta Ti Shang Tao Chün
   太微東霞扶桑丹林大帝上道君
Ting Ling-wei 丁令微
Ts'ai Ching 蔡經
Tung Huang 東皇
Tung Shuang-ch'eng 董雙成
Tung Wang Fu [Kung] 東王父〔公〕
Tzu Yang Chün 紫陽君
Wang Tzu-chin 王子晉
Wei Shu-ch'ing 衛叔卿
Yao 堯
Yen Ching-chu 煙景珠
Yü Huang 玉皇

HUMANS

Ch'in Shih Huang Ti 秦始皇帝
Chou Ling Wang 周靈王
Han Wu Ti 漢武帝
Hsü (brothers) 許
Huang Ch'ao 黃巢
I Tsung 懿宗
Li Lung-chi 李隆基
Liu Ch'e 劉徹
T'ang Hsüan Tsung 唐玄宗
Tung-fang Shuo 東方朔
Wang Chien 王建

Yang Hsi 楊羲
Yang Kuei-fei 楊貴妃
Yao-pin 堯賓

TITLES

Chin t'ung 金童
Ling fei 靈妃
San kuan pao ming 三官保命
Szu ming 司命
Shih nü 侍女
Ts'ai nü 采女
Tzu ch'en chih t'ung 紫晨之童
Yü ch'en chih t'ung 玉晨之童
Yü fei 玉妃
Yü nü 玉女

PLACES

Chang Hai 漲海
Ch'ang-an 長安
Ch'eng-tu 成都
Fang-chu 方諸
Fang Hu 方壺
Fu-sang 扶桑
Heng Shan 衡山
Hsi Hua 西華
Hsin-chou 信州
Hua (Shan) 華（山）
Jun-chou 潤州
Kuai-chi 會稽
Kuei-chou 桂州
K'un Lang 崑閬
K'un-lun 崑崙
Lang Feng 閬風
Lang Yüan 閬苑
Liu-chou 柳州
Lo-fou 羅浮
Mao Shan 茅山
Ming Hai 溟海
P'eng Ch'iu 蓬丘
P'eng Hsüan Tung T'ien 蓬玄洞天
P'eng Hu 蓬壺
P'eng-lai 蓬萊

Pi Hai 碧海
Po Hai 渤海
Shang Ch'ing 上清
Shao-hsing 紹興
Shu 蜀
Ta Lo T'ien 大羅天
T'ai Chi 太極
T'ai Ch'ing 太清
T'ai Hsüan Tu 太玄都
T'ai Hu 太湖
Tan Hsia T'ien 丹霞天
T'ang Ku 湯谷
T'ao Yüan 桃源
T'ien T'ai (Shan) 天台（山）
Ts'ang Hai 滄海
Tung Hua (Shan) 東華（山）
Wang Wu (Shan) 王屋（山）
Wu Yüeh 五嶽
Wu-Yüeh 吳越
Yü Ching Shan 玉京山
Yü Ch'ing 玉清
Yü-hang 餘杭
Yün Lai 雲來

EDIFICES

Ch'ing Yüan Fu 青元府
Ch'ing Yüan Kung 清元宮
Fang-chu Kung 方諸宮
K'ai Yüan Szu 開元寺
Lin Hsiao Shih 琳霄室
Ming T'ang 明堂
T'ai I T'an 太一壇
T'ai Wei Kung 太微宮
Tan Ch'üeh Huang Fang 丹闕黃房
T'ang Ch'ang Kuan 唐昌觀
Tzu Chu Hsüan Fu 紫珠玄府
Yü Fei T'ai Chen Yüan 玉妃太真院
Yün Ching Ch'üeh 雲景闕

WRITINGS

Ch'ang hen ko 長恨歌
Chen kao 真誥

Ch'u tz'u 楚辭
Chuang tzu 莊子
Hai yao pen ts'ao 海藥本草
Hua chien chi 花間集
Huai nan tzu 淮南子
Huang t'ing ching 黃庭經
Lao tzu 老子
Mu t'ien tzu chuan 穆天子傳
Pa su chang 八素章
Shan hai ching 山海經
Sou shen chi 搜神記
Tao tsang 道藏
Yu hsien [shih] 游仙〔詩〕
Yüeh fu 樂府

WORDS

ao 鼇
*bung-bwĕt 潏浡 = 滭浡
ch'e ao 車螯
ch'en 晨,辰
chen (jen) 真〔人〕
ch'en lou 晨樓
ch'i 氣
chiang 絳
chiao 蛟
chin kang 金剛
chin shih 進士
ching 景
ching po 鯨波
ch'iung 瓊
fu ti 福地
hsia 霞
hsiang 象
hsiao 簫
hsien 仙
hsien tzu 仙子
hsing-hsing hsüeh 猩猩血
hsü wu 虛無
hsüan 玄
hua chi 化機
lai 萊
li hua ch'un 梨花春

ling 靈
luan 鸞
lung 龍
p'eng (windblown hair) 鬅
p'eng (sail) 蓬
p'eng-po; see **bung-bwĕt*
pi 碧
p'ing-p'eng 萍蓬
po (**bwĕt*) 孛, 勃, 渤
se-se 瑟瑟
shang 商
t'ai 太
t'ai hun 太混
t'ai meng 太濛
t'ai yüan 太淵
t'ai yün 太蘊
tan ch'ing 丹青

ti ching 地鏡
t'ien pao 天寶
ts'ai yün 采雲
ts'ang 滄
tung hsiao 洞簫
tung t'ien 洞天
tzu ch'iung 紫瓊
tzu chu 紫珠
tz'u 詞
yang 陽
yao 瑤
yin 陰
yin huo 陰火
yü jen 羽人
yü jui 玉蕊
yüan ch'i 元氣
yüeh 嶽

Index

Note: Some subjects are so pervasive in this book that they have not been indexed. They include: Love, Masque(rade), Poetry, Religion, T'ang, Taoism, Ts'ao T'ang.

Alchemy, 14–15, 34, 35, 67, 78, 109, 115
Alligator, 84
Aloeswood, 60
An-ch'i (Sheng), 38, 52, 53
Ao (giant turtle), 89. *See also* Turtle
Ao (lithophone), 40
Apricot, 44, 91, 119
Astral essences, as sources of vitality. *See* Moon; Stars; Sun
Aurora, auroral, 19, 24, 36, 54, 95, 104, 110, 111, 119
Autumn, 45, 63, 96, 99, 109. *See also* Spring; Time; Transience; Winter

Bird woman, 93–94, 101
Blue Lad, 40, 52, 72, 77, 93, 100, 105, 107, 108–121
Blue Woman, 73
Blue-waisted Jade Woman, 73
Buddhism, Buddhist, 9, 32, 114

Calabash, as miniature cosmos, 61–65
Callicarpa dichotoma, 107
Candle, wax, 87
Canton, 85
Capeline Cantos. See *Nü kuan tz'u*
Cave, cavern. *See* Grotto
Chang-hai, 55

Ch'ang-an, 9, 63, 101
Che hsien yüan, 12
Chekiang, 34, 92, 94, 112
Chen (jen). See Realized (Person)
Chen kao, 14, 110, 112, 113, 114
Chen Yu-hsiao, 68
Ch'en. See Clam-monster
Ch'en Hung, 68
Ch'en lou. See Clam Castle
Ch'en T'ao, 56
Ch'en Ts'ang-ch'i, 89
Ch'eng-tu, 9
Ch'i, 87. *See also* Pneuma
Chia Pao-an, 60
Chiang Shu-mao, 60
Ch'ien Ch'i, 85
Ch'ien Liu, 60
Ch'in, 38, 52
Ch'in shih huang ti. See Inaugural Resplendent Thearch of Ch'in
Ch'ing T'ung. See Blue Lad
Ch'ing yüan fu (Archive of the Blue Prime), 109
Ch'ing yüan kung (Palace of Clarified Prime), 104
Chiu hsia, 18
Chiu t'ien chen wang, 60
Ch'iung "rose-gem," 25
Chou, 37
Chou I-shan, 111
Chou Ling wang (Numinous King of Chou), 38
Chou Pi-ta, 101

Ch'u tz'u, 13, 14
Ch'üan T'ang shih, 32–33
Chuang tzu, 3, 14, 58, 59
Ch'un Wen-ch'i, 72, 115
Cinnabar, 36, 95, 104
Cinnamon, 112
Clam Castle, 80–89
Clam-monster, 58, 80–89. *See also* Kraken
Color, 23–24, 54, 108–109. *See also* Cinnabar; Purple
Comet, 55
Confucius, 74
Coral, 59
Corruption, corruptible, 23, 33, 45. *See also* Mortality; Transience
Cosmic egg, 59, 62
Cosmology, 16–19
Cosmos in miniature (as grotto, calabash), 61–65
Costume, 36, 67, 74–79; of feathers, 113
Crane, 38, 74, 93, 94, 96, 98, 99, 100, 101, 120
Counterpart, 19
Cyan Sea, 76, 104, 116
Cycle, Cosmic, 76, 94, 95, 96; of 3000 years, 53, 106. *See also* Mulberry Fields; Time

Darwin, Erasmus, 46–47
Dipper (Northern, Starry), 33, 69, 91, 112
Divine Woman, 12
Dragon, 15, 58, 62, 64, 70, 81–82, 100, 109, 111, 112, 116, 117, 118, 120

East Stygia, 91, 100
Eastern Florescence, 105, 113,

116. *See also* Western Florescence
Eastern Sea, 53, 54, 73, 79, 84, 91, 92, 93, 96, 97, 100, 103. *See also* Cyan Sea; Stygian Sea; Watchet Sea
Elixir, 54, 70, 75, 91, 113
Elysian Isles. *See* P'eng-lai

Fang-chu (Island, Palace), 76, 104, 108–121
Fang hu, 62. *See also* P'eng-lai
Fata Morgana, 80–89. *See also* Mirage
Five Marchmounts, 76. *See also* Marchmount
Five Planets, 74
Flowers, 44–45, 64, 100–101. *See also* Transience
Frost, 73
Fu-sang, 52, 54, 103–107, 108

Garden, 34, 35, 41, 45, 46, 60, 100, 101, 111
Gold, 79, 104
Gourd, 65, 97. *See also* Calabash
Grand Clarity (*T'ai ch'ing*), 22
Grand Culmen, Grand Culmination. *See* *T'ai chi*
Grand Monad, Altar of, 33
Grand Subtlety, 104
Grand Void, 17, 18. *See also* *T'ai hsü*
Grotto (limestone cavern), 15, 39, 41–42, 44, 64, 65, 69, 81, 94, 95, 114
Grotto Heaven, 34, 61, 64, 111
Gulf of Tonkin, 83

Hai nei shih chou chi, 14
Hai yao pen ts'ao, 13

Hainan, 60
Hall of Light (*Ming T'ang*), 6
Han, 13, 21, 23, 25, 52, 53, 87, 88,
    105
Han Wu Ti, 33, 37; and Lady Li,
    34
Han Wu ti nei chuan, 14
Han Yü, 68
Hangchou, 91
Heavenly Masters (Chang), 3
Heng, Mount, 34
Highest Clarity, 4, 5, 6, 8, 9, 15,
    21, 22, 39, 60, 64, 68, 77, 95,
    106, 109, 114. *See also* Mao
    Shan; *Shang ch'ing*
Ho tu shen, 12
Hsi Wang Mu, 40, 68, 118. *See
    also* Royal Mother of the West
Hsiao Shih, 33, 38, 117, 121
Hsiao yu hsien shih, 32
Hsien (transcendent), 12
Hsin-chou, 32
Hsü (Mi and Hui), 69
Hsü Ching-tsung, 87
Hsü Hun, 9
Hsü Ning, 89
Hsüeh T'ao, 9
Hu Kung (Sire of the Pot), 97
Hua, Mount, 68, 70
Hua chien chi, 11, 13
Huai nan tzu, 82
Huang Ch'ao, 10
Huang t'ing ching, 6, 14. *See also*
    Scripture of the Yellow Court

I Tsung (Li Ts'ui), 87
Iconography. *See* Costume
Inaugural Resplendent Thearch of
    Ch'in, 38
India, Indies, 55, 58
Iran, 58

Jade, 79, 104, 119
Jade Capital, Mountain of the (*Yü
    ching shan*), 73
Jade Clarity, 17, 22, 23, 63, 118
Jade Consort, 67–70, 77, 115. *See
    also* Jade Woman
Jade Consort of Eastern Flores-
    cence, 72. *See also* Eastern
    Florescence
Jade Esquire, 76
Jade Maiden. *See* Jade Woman
Jade Resplendent One (*Yü
    huang*), 74, 75, 106
Jade Stamens, 100–102
Jade Woman, 8, 21, 22, 32, 34, 36,
    40, 64, 71–76, 101, 106, 114,
    115, 116, 117. *See also* Jade
    Consort
Jade Woman of Greatest Mystery,
    72
Jade Woman of Occult Miracles,
    72
Japan, Japanese, 54, 85, 89
Ju meng ling, 12
Juan Chao, 32, 33, 38–39, 42, 74,
    75, 117, 118
Juan lang kuei, 12
Jujube, 38, 52, 53
Jun-chou, 9
Jupiter (planet), 38

K'ai Yüan Szu, 32
K'ang P'ien, 101
Kao T'ang fu, 12
Kiangsi, 32, 94, 95
Ko Hung, 34
Korea, 83, 85
Kraken, 77, 79, 82–84. *See also*
    Clam-monster
Ku K'uang, 8
Kuai-chi, 112

Kudzu (flower), 45
Kuei tien ch'iu, 12
K'un-lun, 51, 52, 53, 59, 62, 68,
    88, 99, 107, 117; and *hun-t'un*,
    128–129*n*33. *See also* Royal
    Mother of the West
Kuo P'u, 14
Kuo Szu-ch'ao, 69
Kwangsi, 31
Kwangtung, 52, 76

Lady of Highest Prime, 40, 77, 92
Lady of Southern Marchmount,
    105
Lang Feng, 62. *See also* K'un-lun
Lao tzu, 3. *See also* Lord Lao
Lao tzu (text), 3, 4, 14
Li Hsün, 13
Li Lung-chi, 68. *See also* T'ang
    Hsüan Tsung
Li Po, 7, 8, 57, 62, 78, 109
Li Shang-yin, 86, 88
Liaotung, 96, 98, 120
Lieh hsien chuan, 14
Lin chiang hsien, 12
Ling Pao, 4
Lithophone, 95, 107. See also *Ao*
Liu Ch'e, 98. *See also* Han Wu Ti
Liu Ch'en, 32, 33, 38–39, 42, 43,
    117, 118
Liu Yü-hsi, 9, 101
Lo-fou, Mount, 34, 52, 76
Lo Kiang-hsü, 60
Lo Yin, 31
Lord Lao, 72. *See also* Lao tzu
Lu Kuei-meng, 9, 10, 69
Luminescence, 22, 59. *See also*
    Phosphorescence
Lung-yü, 33

Ma Ku. *See* Miss Hemp

Ma Tai, 9
Mahler, Gustav, 46
Manchuria, 96
Manchus, 2
Mao (brothers), 69, 77. *See also*
    Mao Chung; Mao Ying
Mao Chung, 39
Mao Shan, 4–6, 8, 9, 14, 21, 39, 69,
    76, 77, 86, 104, 106, 108, 111;
    Patriarch, 8
Mao Ying, 5, 77
Marchmount, 19, 68
Martial Thearch of Han, 37, 38,
    53, 117. *See also* Han Wu Ti
Melon, 59
Metropolis of Greatest Mystery
    (*T'ai hsüan tu*), 73
Mica, 98
Milky Way. *See* Sky River
Ming t'ang. See Hall of Light
Mirage, 63–64, 65, 77. *See also*
    Fata Morgana
Mirror, 109–110
Miss Hemp, 33, 90–102
Moon, 109–111, 113; as source of
    vitality, 106, 110; fairies, 68
Mortality, 37, 46, 96. *See also* Cor-
    ruption; Transience
Mu t'ien tzu. See Tranquil Son of
    Heaven
Mu t'ien tzu chuan, 14
Mulberry, 95, 99, 100, 104
Mulberry Fields (Plantations), 92,
    96, 97, 115
Mushroom, 54, 113, 118
Music, 65, 107, 121; and cosmic
    cycles, 36. *See also*
    Lithophone; Reed-organ;
    Syrinx; Time; Transience
Music Archive, 12, 13. *See also*
    Yüeh fu

Nan hsiang tzu, 13
Nan Yüeh fu-jen. *See* Lady of
    Southern Marchmount
Nanking, 4, 5, 101
Nine Songs (*Chiu ko*), 112
North, as realm of ghosts, 45, 73
Numen, Numinous, 19–20
Nü kuan tzu, 12, 42, 43–44

Offenbach, 46
Ou-yang Chiung, 13

Pa su chang, 106
Pacing the Void, 14, 44, 65; Can-
    tos on, 9. *See also Pu hsü (tz'u)*
Panpipes, 78, 111. *See also* Syrinx
Paradise. *See* Garden
Peach (tree, flower, fruit), 39, 42,
    43, 59, 96, 99
Peaches, Font of, 74, 75. *See also*
    Juan Chao; Liu Ch'en
Pear, 100
Pearl, 93
P'ei Tu, 9
*P'eng (*bung)* "wind-tossed tan-
    gle," 55, 57
P'eng ch'iu, 56
P'eng-lai, 36, 38 51–60, 61 62, 63,
    65, 76, 79, 88–89, 90, 92, 94,
    95, 98, 99, 101, 103, 112, 114
*P'eng-po (*bung-bwět)* "bursting
    water," 55
Peri, 58
Persian, 13
Phosphor, 20, 78
Phosphorescence, 34, 36, 83. *See
    also* Luminescence
Pi Ch'ang-fang, 97
P'i Jih-hsiu, 9, 57, 86
P'ing-p'eng "nuphar," 56
Pinikon, 84

Pneuma, 20, 114. *See also Ch'i*
*Po (*bwět)* "pop," 54–55
Po Chü-i, 9, 68, 101
Po-hai, 54
Pole, Pole Star, Polar Palace, 75,
    105
Priestess, 42, 117
Primal Pneuma, 17, 20, 21, 59, 63.
    See also Yüan ch'i
Prose fiction. *See* Wonder tales
Pu hsü (tz'u), 13. *See also* Pacing
    the Void
Purple, 75
Purple Tenuity, Palace of (*Tzu
    wei kung*), 104

Realized (Person), 21, 41, 60, 105
Reed-organ, 38, 40
Rose-gem. *See Ch'iung*
Royal Father of the East, 105
Royal Mother of the West, 33, 37,
    38, 40, 53, 57, 68–69, 70, 78,
    91, 99, 105, 106, 107, 112, 114,
    116, 119. *See also* Hsi Wang
    Mu

Sacred Mountain, 62, 70. *See also*
    Marchmount
Saunters in Sylphdom, 17, 33, 35,
    41, 44, 110. *See also Hsiao yu
    hsien shih*; *Ta yu hsien shih*; *Yu
    hsien*
Scripture of the Yellow Court, 6.
    See also Huang t'ing ching
Scriptures, 71
Sea-isle, Seamount, 35, 56, 59, 88,
    101, 110
Seven Realized Ones (*Ch'i chen*),
    69
Shan hai ching, 14
Shang (myxolydian, mode of

autumn), 99
Shang ch'ing, 4. See also Highest
    Clarity; Mao Shan
Shang Yüan fu-jen, 40. See also
    Lady of Highest Prime
Shao-hsing, 60
Shen hsien chuan, 14
Shen nü fu, 12
Shih i chi, 14
Shu, 10. See also Szechwan
Silk, kraken, 77, 79, 83–84
Six Dynasties, 12
Sky River, 33
Snow, 73, 96, 97
Sou shen chi, 14
South China Sea, 55, 83, 85
South Culmen (Nan chi), 91
Spring, 45, 57, 62, 99, 100. See also
    Autumn; Time; Transience
Star women, 70
Stars, as sources of vitality, 57
Stygian Sea, 53–54, 104. See also
    East Stygia
Su Lin, 76
Sun, 103, 104, 107; as source of
    vitality, 106, 110
Sung, 4, 95, 101
Sung Ch'en-yang, 60
Sung Yü, 12, 14
Sword, magic, 78
Sylph. See Transcendent
Syrinx, 33, 38, 99, 115, 120, 121
Szechwan, Szechwanese, 13. See
    also Shu
Szu-ma Ch'eng-chen, 8
Szu ming (Supervisor of Destiny),
    115

Ta Ch'in, 14
Ta lo t'ien, 17
Ta yu hsien shih, 32

T'ai chi, 63, 76, 115
T'ai hsü, 17. See also Grand Void
T'ai Hu, 9, 58
T'ai i t'an, 33
T'ai wei. See Grand Subtlety
T'ai yin (Grand Yin), 110,
    135n147
Taiwan, 13
T'ang ch'ang kuan (Belvedere of
    T'ang's Glory), 101
T'ang Hsüan Tsung, 68. See also
    Li Lung-chi
T'ang ku. See Valley of Thermae
Tangerine, 76
Tao tsang, 3
Thearch, 22. See also Ti
Theocracy, 4
Ti "thearch," 124n35
T'ien hsien tzu, 11–12
T'ien T'ai, 32, 33, 38, 39, 42, 43,
    44, 62, 75, 94, 95, 117
Time, 45; relativity of cosmic and
    earthly, 39. See also Cycle;
    Transience
Ting Ling-wei, 96
Tranquil Son of Heaven, 33, 37,
    117
Transcendent, 21, 22, 36, 41, 54,
    60, 85, 89, 94, 100, 106, 113,
    115, 120. See also Hsien; Peri
Transience, 36, 42, 46, 63, 96;
    flowers as symbols of, 44, 53;
    water as symbol of, 43, 74. See
    also Apricot; Corruption;
    Flowers; Kudzu; Mortality;
    Mulberry; Peach; Pear; Time
Ts'ai Ching, 91–93, 95
Ts'ang Hai. See Watchet Sea
Ts'ao Chih, 14
Tu Fu, 85
Tu Kuang-t'ing, 10, 88

Tu Mu, 9
Tumbleweed, 56, 95
Tumbleweed Pot, 61, 62
Tung huang (Resplendent One of the East), 118
Tung Shuang-ch'eng, 40
Tung-fang Shuo, 38
Tung-t'ing, Lake, 84
Turtle, 56, 57, 58. See also Ao (giant turtle)
Turtle Mother, 57
Tzu chu hsüan fu, 32
Tzu wei. See Purple Tenuity
Tzu yang chün (Lord of Purple Solarity), 111
Tz'u, 42

Valley of Thermae, 104
Venus (planet), 8, 38
Vermilion Palace, 73
Vietnamese, 83

Wang Ch'iao, 38
Wang Chien, 10
Wang Tzu-ch'iao, 74, 117. See also Wang Tzu-chin
Wang Tzu-chin, 38
Wang Wei, 87
Wang Wu, Mount, 8
Wang Yüan, 33, 91–92, 95
Watchet, 24, 54
Watchet Sea, 54, 77, 92, 93, 94, 100. See also Cyan Sea; Eastern Sea; Stygian Sea
Water, 64–65
Weaving Woman, 33
Wei, Northern, 4
Wei Ch'ü-mou, 8–9, 13
Wei Shu-ch'ing, 98
Wei Ying-wu, 59

Western Florescence, 68, 116. See also Eastern Florescence
Whales, 84–85
White Stone Mountain, 115
Winter, 96, 120
Wonder tales, 10, 14, 52, 87
Wu shan i tuan yün, 12, 13
Wu shan kao, 12
Wu-Yüeh, 60
Wu Yün, 8, 9, 13, 14, 17, 44, 54, 62

Yang, 18, 20, 35, 54, 62, 63, 70, 91, 95, 96, 101, 105, 106, 110, 116
Yang Hsi, 69, 106
Yang Kuei-fei, 68
Yangtze (River Valley), 5, 9
Yao (mythical hero), 96, 97
Yao "azure-gem," 25
Yen Chen-ch'ing, 8, 94, 95
Yen Ching-chu, 72, 115
Yen Hsiu-fu, 101
Yin, 20, 35, 62, 63, 70, 83, 95, 96, 106, 109, 110, 116
Yu hsien, 13, 14, 46. See also Hsiao yu hsien shih; Saunters in Sylphdom; Ta yu hsien shih
Yu ming lu, 14
Yü ch'ing. See Jade Clarity
Yü-hang, 91
Yü Hsüan-chi, 9
Yü huang. See Jade Resplendent One
Yüan Chen, 9, 101
Yüan ch'i, 17, 20. See also Primal Pneuma
Yüeh fu, 12. See also Music Archive
Yün Lai, 56

Zither, 99

Designer:	Mark Ong
Compositor:	Asco Trade Typesetting Ltd.
Text:	Garamond
Display:	Palatino and Garamond
Printer:	Edwards Brothers Inc.
Binder:	Edwards Brothers Inc.